THE CASE FOR
THE
SECOND COMING
OF
CHRIST

AN INVESTIGATION
INTO THE
BIBLICAL EVIDENCE

DANIEL DERY

Published by:
JaDon Management Inc.
1405 4th Ave. N. W.
#109
Ardmore, Ok. 73401

Cover Design by
Jeffrey T. McCormack
The Pendragon: Web and Graphic Design
www.the pendragon.net

DEDICATED:

To all who will choose scripture over tradition, and engage in the battle to reform biblical eschatology back into its original image; covenant eschatology, thank you.

> *"Holding fast the faithful word which is in accordance with the teaching, so that he will be able both to exhort in sound doctrine and to refute those who contradict."*   *Titus 1:9*

FOREWORD

Once again, Daniel Dery has produced an outstanding book demonstrating, beyond doubt, that the "Second Coming" of Christ was not only predicted to be in the first century, at the fall of Jerusalem, but that it did take place, vindicating Jesus as the Son of God and his apostles as inspired authors. This is an important book for all students of the Bible, and especially those interested in "eschatology" i.e. a study of the "last things."

Dery methodically, logically, and convincingly shows the correlation between the words of Jesus, the Old Covenant prophets and the New Testament writers, showing their perfect harmony both as to the nature and the timing of that event. I particularly appreciate his extensive comments and work on Daniel. While some would decry and deny that much of Daniel contains Messianic prophecy of Jesus, Dery's examination, and illustration through some great charts, puts the lie to those claims. Over and over Dery presents a convincing case for the Messianic application of Daniel by the New Testament writers.

Not only that, Dery effectively and powerfully shows the utter inconsistency of Bible students who appeal to text after text for proof of the Second Coming of Christ, but, those same commentators reject, distort, mitigate, elasticize and deny the time element found in the very passages that they appeal to for the fact of the Second Coming. Dery correctly notes that incredible inconsistency of this approach.

Finally, as a Bible student dedicated to understanding the New Testament use and application of the Old Testament, I greatly appreciate how Dery, shows, with mastery, how key New Testament prophecies of the "time of the end" are citations of key Old Testament prophecies that unequivocally posit the end at the end of the Old Covenant aeon, that arrived at the fall of Jerusalem in AD 70. Once again, his work on Daniel is outstanding in this regard. This is some powerful exegetical material that every Bible student needs to read and ponder.

Jadon Management was proud to publish Dan Dery's first book, *The Transition Between Two Covenants.* It is an excellent book, and I highly recommend it. We are equally honored to be able to publish this second book by Dan Dery. It is *outstanding* and needs to find a place in the library of every Bible student.

Don K. Preston (D. Div.)
President, Preterist Research Institute
Author of 25 Books on Eschatology.
www.donkpreston.com
www.bibleprophecy.com

A WORD FROM THE AUTHOR

On any short list of the most important and debated doctrines of the New Testament, the second coming of Christ would most assuredly appear near the top. Misunderstandings concerning the "time" (past or future) and the "nature" (natural or spiritual) of this fundamental doctrine have been the source of much confusion in the field of biblical eschatology for the past two millennia. Prior to AD70, scoffers were denying that the Lord would return in the first century according to his promise (Matthew 16:27-28, 24:30-34, 2 Peter 3:3-4). Today, the followers of those same scoffers are still denying the fulfillment of that promise.

I am convinced that as we proceed through this book the reader will be amazed by how plainly and consistently this doctrine is taught throughout the pages of scripture. The message of the return of the King in glory was not whispered in a corner, nor was it uttered in riddles, but was proclaimed into all the world as the gospel of the kingdom of God, and was promised to find fulfillment within the lifetime of Christ's first disciples. If you are not yet familiar with the following passage, you will be in short order.

> For the Son of Man is going to come in the glory of His Father with His angels, and will then repay every man according to his deeds. Truly I say to you, there are some of those who are standing here who will not taste death until they see the Son of Man coming in His kingdom.   Matthew 16:27-28

As we present our case for a first century second coming of Christ through an investigation into the biblical evidence, we invite you on a most challenging, yet most rewarding journey. I hope you will join us.

CONTENTS OF THE BOOK

PART I:
AN INTRODUCTION

1-2   Let us Prepare our Hearts
3-10   His Appearing Out of The Second
11-12   A Key to Proper Interpretation
13-17   Confusion Within the Camps

PART II:
IDENTIFYING THE PRIMARY PROPHETIC
SOURCES FOR MATTHEW 16:27-28

19-22   Keeping it in Context
23   Stating the Argument
24-28   Matthew 16:27-28 = Daniel 7:13-14
29-32   A Closer Look at Daniel 7 - Time, Times and a Half a Time
33-35   When the Saints Took Possession of the Kingdom
36-40   Israel the Lord's Vineyard
41-42   Removing what can be Shaken
43-45   Daniel 7 & Revelation 19-20
46-49   Matthew 16:27-28 = Isaiah 59:17-21
50-54   A Closer Look at Isaiah 59 - Vengeance for Shedding Innocent Blood
55-59   The Day of Salvation
60-65   The Arrival of the New Covenant
66-67   Matthew 16:27-28 = Isaiah 40:10 & Isaiah 62:11
68-70   Isaiah, The Baptist and the Gospel of the Kingdom
71-76   John, Malachi, and the Time of Harvest
77-81   A Closer Look at Isaiah 40 - The Gathering of Israel
82-89   A Closer Look at Isaiah 62 - The Messianic Remarriage
90-92   The Marriage and the Message of John
93-94   Part II Conclusion

PART III:
MATTHEW 16:27-28 - A PRIMARY PROPHETIC SOURCE FOR THE
SECOND COMING OF CHRIST IN THE NEW TESTAEMNT

97   Stating the Argument
98-102   Matthew 16:27-28 = Revelation 22:12
103-104   A Closer Look at Revelation 22:12 - The Great White Throne Judgment
105-107   Matthew 16:27-28 = Revelation 1:7
108-111   A Closer Look at Revelation 1:7 - Matthew 26:64 & More
112-115   Matthew 16:27-28 = Matthew 24 & 25 - The Olivet Discourse
116-117   A Closer Look at The Olivet Discourse - The Great Trumpet of God
118-120   Matthew 16:27-28 = Matthew 13 - The Wheat & The Tares
121-124   A Closer Look at Matthew 13 - The Harvest & The End of the Age
125-129   Matthew 16:27-28 = 1 Thessalonians 4:15-17
130-132   A Closer Look at 1 Thessalonians 4 - The Resurrection of 1 Corinthians 15

133-136   Matthew 16:27-28 = 2 Thessalonians 1:4-10
137-140   A Closer Look at 2 Thessalonians 1 - Zephaniah & the Day of the Lord
141-144   Isaiah & Flames of Fire
145-148   Matthew 16:27-28 = 2 Timothy 4:1
149-150   A Closer Look at 2 Timothy 4 - Alexander the Coppersmith
151-153   Part III Conclusion

PART IV:
THE HISTORICAL SUPPORT OF THE BIBLICAL TRUTH

155-156   The Testimony of Two or Three Witnesses
157-162   Angelic Armies Seen in the Clouds - Lyar (April) 21, AD66
163-166   A Voice Heard from the Temple - June AD66 - Pentecost
167-168   Case Closed: Matthew 16:27-28 - The Second Coming of Christ Fulfilled in AD70

PART I

AN INTRODUCTION

LET US PREPARE OUR HEARTS

Before we begin such a challenging yet rewarding task, I think it only fitting and responsible to renew and affirm both our commitment and submission to the inspired and infallible words of scripture, as did those who came before us. May we not take these words lightly as many have done and continue to do in our days.

The Belgic Confession - Article 5
The Authority of Scripture

"We receive all these books and these only as holy and canonical, for the regulating, founding, and establishing of our faith. And *we believe without a doubt all things contained in them....*"

The Belgic Confession - Article 7
The Sufficiency of Scripture

".... For since it is forbidden to add to the Word of God, or take anything away from it, it is plainly demonstrated that the teaching is perfect and complete in all respects. Therefore, we must not consider human writings - no matter how holy their authors may have been - equal to the divine writings; nor may   we put custom, nor the majority, nor age, nor the passage of times or persons, nor councils, decrees, or official decisions above the truth of God, for truth is above everything else.... *Therefore, we reject with all our hearts everything that does not agree with this infallible rule....*"

The Westminster Confession of Faith - Chapter 1

"The infallible rule of interpretation of Scripture is the Scripture itself: and therefore, when there is a question about the true and full sense of any Scripture (which is not manifold, but one), it must be searched and known by other places that speak more clearly.... *The best and only infallible rule of interpretation of Scripture, is the Scripture itself.* Some things that are briefly and obscurely handled in one place, are more fully and clearly explained in other places; and, therefore, *when we would find out the true sense of Scripture, we must compare one passage with another, that they may illustrate one another....*"

It is in the spirit of these confessions that I stand immovable in my belief based on scripture alone, that the second coming of Christ was accomplished in the first century, in the lifetime of Jesus' contemporary disciples. I consider the clear testimony of scripture concerning the *time* of that coming as infallible doctrine, and reject completely any doctrine, creed, or tradition of man which *plainly contradicts* the consistent teaching of Christ and his apostles on this matter. Throughout this book, we will consistently apply the "infallible rule of interpretation" - that scripture interprets scripture - to demonstrate and thus establish the first century fulfillment of the second coming of Christ. Let's begin with the promise of his reappearing.

HIS APPEARING OUT OF THE SECOND

Hebrews 9:28
So Christ also, having been offered once to bear the sins of many, *will appear a second time for salvation* without reference to sin, to those who eagerly await Him.

As far as I can tell, it is from this verse that the popular phrase "the second coming" primarily originates. Although the concept is valid, the phrase itself does not exist within the canon of scripture.1 Below is my working definition of what has come to be known as the second coming, or, the Parousia 2 of Christ.

"The final and redemptive return of the covenant-presence of Yahweh to fulfill all prophecy including the final resurrection and judgment, and to consummate Israel's salvation and return from covenant-exile by establishing his eternal rule and reign (his kingdom) in their midst".

Regardless of whether you agree with this definition or not, what remains an undeniable biblical fact is this: The first disciples of Christ eagerly expected the fulfillment of his second coming based on the promise of Jesus himself. Indeed, it is impossible to read through the gospels and not see in Jesus's teachings a dominant emphasis on his coming (return) in glory. Likewise, one can hardly read a letter in the New Testament without finding his apostles, according to his promise, proclaiming that same message. The following are just a few of the more obvious scriptures which support the New Testament doctrine of the

---

1. The literal reading of this phrase in Hebrews 9:28 is, "shall appear *out of second*". In the context of Hebrews 9, the appearing of Christ "out of second" was his high-priestly return from the most holy place - the second tabernacle - in completion of the atonement. The day of atonement imagery in Hebrews 9 is taken directly from Leviticus 16. My gratitude to Don K. Preston and Sam Dawson for bringing these truths to my attention.
2. Although it is not used in all "second coming texts" in the New Testament, the Greek word "Parousia" has become synonymous with the second coming of Christ. According to Eerdmans Dictionary of the Bible, the word Parousia is a Greek noun, used of persons or things, meaning "arrival" or "active presence", from the verb *pareimi*, "to be present". Vines Expository Dictionary of New Testament Words says that Parousia denotes "both an arrival and a consequent presence with". Thus, the Parousia of Christ was the arrival - the return - of his covenant-presence among his people.

3

second coming of Christ. There is a general consensus among most futurists that these passages do prophesy that great event.3

> John 14:2-3
> In My Father's house are many dwelling places; if it were not so, I would have told you; for *I go to prepare a place for you.* If I go and prepare a place for you, *I will come again and receive you to Myself,* that where I am, there you may be also.

> Acts 1:9,11
> And after He had said these things, He was lifted up while they were looking on, and a cloud received Him out of their sight.... They also said, "Men of Galilee, why do you stand looking into the sky? *This Jesus, who has been taken up from you into heaven, will come in just the same way as you have watched Him go into heaven."*

> Acts 3:19-21
> Therefore, repent and return, so that your sins may be wiped away, in order that times of refreshing may come from the presence of the Lord; and *that He may send Jesus, the Christ appointed for you, whom heaven must receive until the period of restoration of all things* about which God spoke by the mouth of His holy prophets from ancient time.

> 1 Corinthians 15:22-23
> For as in Adam all die, so also in Christ all will be made alive. But each in his own order: Christ the first fruits, *after that those who are Christ's at His coming.*

Clearly, the doctrine of the second coming of Christ as anticipated by the first century disciples is easily established from scripture, no honest student of truth denies this. Yet significantly, all futurists deny the testimony of scripture concerning *when* both Jesus and his disciples said it was to occur. What is amazing to me is that even though scripture is *equally clear* concerning the second coming itself as well as *the time* of that coming, it is only the latter that is denied or even disputed. A question all futurists would do well to ask themselves is this:

If the unity and harmony of the verses listed above can and does establish the New Testament doctrine of the second coming of Christ, then shouldn't a similar list of unified and harmonious verses which identify *the time* of that coming, hold the same authority to establish *when* that event would take place?

---

3.   For example, Charles R. Erdman - Acts 3:19-21, Matthew Henry - John 14:2- 3, David Brown - Acts 1:9-11, Leon Morris - 1 Corinthians 15:22-23.

The honest answer is yes, and the reality is, such a list does exist; yet for the most part it goes completely ignored by most Christians, and completely abused or denied by most commentators. 4 The statement we made earlier, that Jesus and his first disciples eagerly expected his second coming, although true, only partially communicates their actual expectation. The first century apostolic message and expectation of the second coming of Christ is more accurately defined in the following words:

"Both Jesus and his first century disciples eagerly expected his second coming to occur within the first century; specifically, within the lifetime of their contemporary generation."

The following are just a few of the passages in the New Testament which clearly teach this fundamental and undeniable truth. In all three synoptic gospels, Jesus told his disciples that his second coming was to occur in their lifetime.

> Matthew 10:22-23
> You will be hated by all because of My name, but it is *the one who has endured to the end who will be saved.* But whenever they persecute you in one city, flee to the next; for truly I say to you, *you will not finish going through the cities of Israel until the Son of Man comes.*

> Matthew 24:30,34
> And then the sign of the Son of Man will appear in the sky, and then all the tribes of the earth will mourn, and *they will see the Son of Man coming on the clouds of heaven* with power and great glory.... Truly I say to you, *this generation will not pass away until all these things take place.*

> Mark 13:26,30
> Then *they will see the Son of Man coming in clouds* with great power and glory.... Truly I say to you, *this generation will not pass away until all these things take place.*

> Luke 21:20,27,32
> But *when you see Jerusalem surrounded by armies,* then recognize that her desolation is near.... *Then they will see the Son of man coming in a cloud* with power and great glory.... Truly I say to you, *this generation will not pass away until all things take place.*

---

4. For an example of this see George Eldon Ladd, *A Commentary on the Revelation of John*, (Grand Rapids; Eerdmans, 1972), p.22 and G.R. Beasley-Murray, *The Book of Revelation, New Century Bible Commentary*, (London; Marshall, Morgan, Scott, 1974).

While on trial before the Sanhedrin in approximately 30AD, Jesus also told Caiaphas and those who stood with him that they would see that same event come to pass....

> Matthew 26:64
> Jesus said to him, "You have said it yourself, nevertheless I tell you, hereafter *you will see the Son of Man sitting at the right hand of power, and coming on the clouds of heaven.*"

> Mark 14:62
> And Jesus said, "I am; and *you shall see the Son of man sitting at the right hand of power, and coming with the clouds of heaven.*

In the book of Revelation, John identified the theme of the book by reiterating the words of Christ. Those who pierced him would see him *"coming with the clouds"*.

> Revelation 1:7
> Behold, *he is coming with the clouds, and every eye will see Him, even those who pierced Him;* and all the tribes of the earth will mourn over Him. So it is to be. Amen.

In Paul's epistles to the Thessalonians, he likewise, drawing on the promises of Jesus, told the Thessalonians that not all of them would die, but some would remain alive until the second coming of Christ. At that time, the Thessalonian Christians would receive relief from their then-present persecution, and their persecutors would receive the punishment they so deserved.

> 1 Thessalonians 4:15-17
> For this we say to you by the word of the Lord, that *we who are alive and remain until the coming of the Lord,* will not precede those who have fallen asleep. For *the Lord Himself will descend from heaven* with a shout, with the voice of the archangel and with the trumpet of God, and the dead in Christ will rise first. Then *we who are alive and remain will be caught up together with them in the clouds to meet the Lord in the air,* and so we shall always be with the Lord.

> 2 Thessalonians 1:6-8
> For after all it is only just for God to repay with affliction those who afflict you, and *to give relief to you who are afflicted and to us as well when the Lord Jesus will be revealed from heaven* with His mighty angels in flaming fire, dealing out retribution to those who do not know God and to those who do not obey the gospel of our Lord Jesus.

And, in his first epistle to the Corinthians, Paul specifically tells his first century audience that not all of them would "sleep" (die) before the sounding of the "last trumpet" at the second coming of Christ. Significantly, this passage teaches that resurrection and Parousia are same-time events.

> 1 Corinthians 15:22-23,51-52
> For as in Adam all die, so also in Christ all will be made alive. But each in his own order: *Christ the first fruits, after that those who are Christ's at His coming....* Behold, I tell you a mystery; *we will not all sleep, but we will all be changed,* in a moment, in the twinkling of an eye, at the last trumpet; for the trumpet will sound, and the *dead will be raised imperishable, and we will be changed.*

Many more texts could be added to this short list, but this is sufficient to establish our point. According to the New Testament, the *time* for the fulfillment of the second coming of Christ is consistently placed in the first century generation, specifically, in the lifetime of Jesus' contemporary disciples. Acknowledging this truth, British philosopher and mathematician Bertrand Russell wrote: "For one thing, He certainly thought that His second coming would occur in the clouds of glory before the death of all the people who were living at that time." 5 To deny these inspired texts is to deny one of the most fundamental elements of the second coming itself, namely, *the time of its fulfillment.*

What virtually all futurist schools seem to overlook is that to deny the time of a prophecy, is to deny the prophecy itself. To illustrate this point, imagine for a moment that after the Lord had told Abraham, "I will surely return to you *at this time next year,* and Sarah your wife will have a son", 6 that both Abraham and Sarah denied the *time* of that promise. Ask yourself, would Abraham and Sarah have truly believed the promise? Surely not, but why? Because there was a *time limitation* connected to the promise which they had not believed. Conversely, what if Isaac would not have been born for another *five years*; would God have been faithful his promise? Surely not, but why? Because God *had limited the*

---

5. Bertrand Russell, *Why I Am Not a Christian: And Other Essays on Religion and Related Subjects,* (London; Allen & Unwin/New York; Simon & Schuster, 1957), p.vi. Russell rightly understood Jesus' expectation of his Parousia, yet, his misunderstanding of its *nature* caused him to reject Christianity altogether. I'm sure that many who have followed in his error have fallen into the same snare.
6. Genesis 18:10

promise to an "appointed time", 7 the promise was limited to *"this time next year",* not five years later. For God to fulfill his promise, he had to fulfill the promise *on time.* Likewise, for Abraham and Sarah to exercise faith in the promise and be counted righteous by faith, they had to believe the *time* of its fulfillment.

If this principle was true for Abraham, Sarah and even Yahweh, why not for Christianity today? Why has "biblical orthodoxy" only partially accepted the doctrine of the second coming of Christ"? It is entirely illogical and unbiblical that the second coming itself has retained such a prominent place in church tradition (although at this point anachronistically), yet an incredibly significant element of that doctrine - *the appointed time of its fulfillment* - continues to be completely ignored and even denied.

To magnify this point even further, consider the chart on the following page listing several second coming passages divided into two columns. The center column shows the portion of the texts which does not specify time, the right column shows the portion of the same texts which are clearly *"time sensitive"*; that is, they limit the fulfillment of the prophecy to a specifically appointed time. The power of this chart is that it demonstrates the "cherry picking" that must take place if one is to reject the first century fulfillment of the second coming of Christ. Once again, futurism affirms the coming itself, yet denies the *time* of that coming found within the same context; sometimes even within the very same verse.

---

7. In Romans 9:9, Paul quotes Genesis 18:10,14 and uses the Greek word "kairos", which means *an appointed time,* as opposed to "chronos", which indicates time in general. By applying this prophecy in Genesis to the body of Christ who was at that time suffering birth pains (Matthew 24:8), Paul taught that the *appointed time* for the Lord's return and the birth of a new nation (the seed of Isaac) through a New Covenant (Sarah-Galatians 4) had arrived in his day.

THE TEXT	HIS COMING	THE TIME OF HIS COMING
Matthew 10:23	Before the Son of Man comes	You will not finish.... going through Israel
Matthew 24:30,34	The Son of Man coming on the clouds of heaven	This generation will not pass away until all these things take place
Matthew 26:64	The Son of Man.... coming on the clouds of heaven	You will see...
Mark 13:26,30	The Son of Man coming in clouds	This generation will not pass away until all these things take place
Luke 21:20,27,32	The Son of man coming in a cloud	When you see Jerusalem surrounded by armies.... this generation will not pass away until all things take place.
1 Thessalonians 4:15-17	The coming of the Lord	We who are alive and remain
2 Thessalonians 1:6-8	The Lord Jesus revealed from heaven	When God repays with affliction those who afflict you, and gives relief to you who are afflicted
1 Corinthians 15:22-23	At His coming	We will not all sleep

The utter inconsistency of those who accept the doctrine of the second coming yet deny the first century *time limitation* that inspired scripture has placed upon it, is evident for all to see. The second coming of Christ is indeed a biblical doctrine, but so is its first century fulfillment. If there is one thing that we, the advocates of covenant eschatology 8 have on our side, it is the biblical evidence, and admittedly that is all we need. After all, if inspiration is not enough, then we ask along with the apostles, "to who's words can we turn"? 9

---

8. Covenant eschatology is the doctrine that biblical eschatology concerns the end of the Old Covenant and its age/world, rather than the end of time or the end of the Christian age, both of which have no end (Jeremiah 33:20-21, Ephesians 3:21). For an excellent study of Covenant eschatology see *"Covenant Eschatology: A Comprehensive Overview"*, by Timothy R. King and Jack C. Scott, Jr.
9. John 6:68

As we have briefly demonstrated so far, one of the most basic yet undeniable truths of the New Testament is that Jesus and his first disciples both promised and expected his second coming to occur within the lifetime of their own generation. So, to somewhat repeat myself, I ask again the following question: Why has the vast majority of Christianity in every generation, for nearly fifty generations, continually rejected this cardinal truth? Why have they rejected the *timing* of this great and glorious doctrine?

It seems to me self-evident that the element of time within the doctrine of the second coming of Christ was given to both "confirm the promise", 10 and to demonstrate the faithfulness of God to fulfill his word. However, by denying *time*, inspiration has been called into question, and Jesus has been labelled as just another prophet of Baal. 11   The ultimate tragedy of this rejection is that the very time statements which were given to the righteous as a shield of faith, have now become the sword of the faithless to pierce the side of the Son of God a second time.

---

10. Romans 15:8, 2 Peter 3:4
11. In his book, *"Dead In Their Tracks, Stopping the Liberal/Skeptic Attack on the Bible"*, John Noe demonstrates that Christianity's denial of a first century Parousia according to the words of Jesus is, in his words, "the crack that let the liberals in the door to begin their systematic criticism and dismantling of Scripture with its inevitable bankrupting of the faith." (Quote taken from the back cover of John Noe's book)

A KEY TO PROPER INTERPRETATION

For those familiar with the study of eschatology and specifically the time statements concerning the second coming, you have no doubt noticed in the lists above the peculiar absence of a particularly powerful and important passage. The passage to which I refer is Matthew 16:27-28. Its absence so far has not been an oversight, but intentional. Let's read it together.

> Matthew 16:27-28
> For the Son of Man is going to come in the glory of His Father with His angels, and will then repay every man according to his deeds. Truly I say to you, *there are some of those who are standing here who will not taste death until they see the Son of Man coming in His kingdom.*

Understanding and demonstrating the significance that this passage holds in our investigation of the doctrine of the second coming will be a major focus throughout this book. Rather than performing painstaking exegesis on all or most of the time sensitive second coming texts contained in scripture, 1 we will instead focus our attention primarily on this one particular passage; and of course its parallels. It is my firm conviction that if the infallible rule of interpretation (to allow scripture to interpret scripture) is consistently applied to Matthew 16:27-28 within its contextual framework, only one conclusion is possible.

Matthew 16:27-28 does in fact prophesy the glorious second coming (the Parousia) of Christ as promised in the prophets, and that it did in fact take place in the first century, within the lifetime of Jesus' contemporary generation. It is this conclusion that we will seek to vindicate throughout this book. Carefully and prayerfully consider what the 19th century theologian James Stuart Russell had to say concerning this most significant passage.

This remarkable declaration is of the greatest importance in this discussion, and may be regarded as the key to the right interpretation of the New Testament doctrine of the Parousia. 2

---

1. For an exegesis on many of the "time sensitive" second coming texts in scripture, see James Stuart Russell's book, *"The Parousia, The New Testament Doctrine of Christ's Second Coming". Also see Don K. Preston's book, "the Last Days Identified".*
2. James Stuart Russell, *The Parousia: A Critical Inquiry into The New Testament Doctrine of Our Lord's Second Coming*, (London; T. Fisher Unwin), p.29

He continues….

"This passage alone contains so much important truth respecting the Parousia, that it may be said to cover the whole ground; and, rightly used, will be found to be a key to the true interpretation of the New Testament doctrine on this subject". 3

Although he did not explicitly state why he believed Matthew 16:27-28 was the "key" to understanding the Parousia, except for that, *"it contains so much important truth respecting the Parousia";* Russell's comments are nonetheless extremely insightful. I am personally convinced that if we can establish beyond doubt that Matthew 16:27-28 did in fact prophecy the second coming of Christ, then all futurist eschatology's are false, and the age-long debate regarding the time and nature of the Parousia is forever settled. In what now follows, I will do my best to communicate my reasons for this conviction.

---

3. Ibid., p.32

CONFUSION WITHIN THE CAMPS

Before we begin our investigation into Matthew 16:27-28, I feel it necessary to provide a brief survey of how several futurist expositors from different eschatological paradigms have understood the text, specifically the *time limitation* in verse 28. As you read these commentators, try to identify the significant interpretive element that is common among their otherwise contradictory statements.

Chrysostom, Hilary and others hold that the phrase "until they see the Son of Man coming…" refers to the transfiguration which immediately followed. 1

Grotius, Calvin, Capellus, Wetstein, Ebrard, Alford, and Owen, interpret it as the destruction of Jerusalem and the founding of the Church.2

Dorner sees it as, "the conquests and progress of the gospel."3

De Wette says, "Christ merely predicted the advent of his kingdom", basically agreeing with Grotius and Wetstein.4

Albert Barnes applies it to the day of Pentecost and the founding of the Church.5

J.A. Alexander and John Gill as, "the gradual and progressive establishment of Christ's kingdom", including both Pentecost and the destruction of Jerusalem.6

David Brown says, "the reference, beyond doubt, is to the firm establishment and victorious progress, in the lifetime of some then present, of that new kingdom of Christ, which was destined to work the greatest of all changes on this earth, and be the grand pledge of His final coming in glory."7

Craig L. Blomberg like Hilary, applies Matthew 16:27-28 to the transfiguration

---

1. John Peter Lang, *Commentary on the Holy Scriptures.*
2. Ibid.
3. Ibid.
4. Ibid.
5. Ibid.
6. Ibid.
7. Jamieson, Fausset, & Brown, *Commentary on Matthew 16 – BLB*

and says, "the glory of Jesus' second coming will soon be foreshadowed in his own transfiguration, the very next event described."8

R.T. France rejects the fulfillment of the text in Jesus' transfiguration and says, "the transfiguration hardly amounts to a fulfillment of the Son of Man's coming with his angels to repay every man". France sees the fulfillment of the text in the ascension of Jesus, when he was "raised and vindicated at God's right hand..."9

Donald A. Hagner understands it as, "the Son of Man as gloriously returning in connection with the destruction of Jerusalem", which destruction "may be regarded as an anticipation of the final judgment". For Hagner, for the disciples to see the destruction of Jerusalem was, "in a sense to see the coming of the Son of man in his kingdom."10

Herman Olshausen admits that the phrase "some of them that stand here", "presupposes that the majority of them will have died previous to the event in question", but remains ambiguous in identifying that event when he says, "some refer to this passage to the destruction of Jerusalem in AD70 as a type and an earnest of the final second coming of Christ."11

Ellicott, like Hagner sees verse 28 as "partially" fulfilled in the "judgment which fell upon the Jewish Church, the destruction of the holy city and the temple..." He sees the AD70 event as a "foreshadowing of the great-far-off event", namely, the final second coming of the Lord.12

John Peter Lange interprets Matthew 16:28 to refer to the resurrection of Christ, when he "revealed himself in the midst of his disciples", but interprets verse 27 as a reference to a yet future "second advent", citing verse 26 as its interpretive key. Lange thus separates the "coming" of verse 27 from the "coming" of verse 28 by nearly 2000 years and counting, 13 based on "context".

Matthew Henry, along the lines of J.A. Alexander, interprets Matthew 16:28 as Christ's coming in his own "mediatorial kingdom". For Henry, the "Son of

---

8. NAC, *Commentary on Matthew*
9. NICNT, *Commentary on Matthew*
10. World Biblical Commentary on Matthew
11. Third Millennium Bible comments
12. Ellicott's Commentary for English Readers
13. John Peter Lang, *Commentary on the Holy Scriptures*

Man coming in his Kingdom" should be understood as his, "coming by the pouring out of his Spirit, the planting of the gospel church, the destruction of Jerusalem, the taking away of the place and nation of the Jews..."14

As you can see, there is massive disagreement among the futurist commentators concerning this passage. However, among their differences there is a significant element that is agreed upon, at least in principle. Were you able to identify it? It is *the element of time*. Look at it like this. By interpreting the "Son of Man coming in his kingdom" (16:28) to refer to either the transfiguration, the resurrection, the ascension, Pentecost, or the destruction of Jerusalem in AD70 (even in a typological sense), the theologians above are tacitly stating their belief that the arrival of the kingdom of God was, at the very least, to begin (be initiated) within the lifetime of the first disciples. This is extremely significant!

What this means is, these commentators admit that Jesus' words *"there are some of those who are standing here who will not taste death until..."* did in fact refer to his first century audience, that is, to his contemporary generation. That's why, in one way or another, all these commentators seek to find a first century event that fulfills the "Son of Man coming of the kingdom". This tells us that these commentators recognize they are unable to pull a "linguistic Houdini" on the phrase "there are some of those who are standing here", like they do on "this generation"15 or many of the other time statements in the New Testament. They therefore do their best to find a satisfactory first century explanation for Jesus' words, while at the same time denying that those very words actually prophesied his second coming. What a conundrum!

However, the question must be asked; can the interpretations of the commentators cited above be biblically justified? Can verse 27 be separated from verse 28 by thousands of years in the name of context, thus creating two (or more) "comings" of the Son of Man in the New Testament? If scripture is compared with scripture, is it biblically accurate or consistent to say that the Son of Man came "in the glory of his Father, with his angels" in the first century, yet that event did not fulfill his second coming? Can anyone truly say with a straight face that the coming of the Son of Man to "repay every man according

---

14. Matthew Henry Commentary on Matthew 14 - BLB
15. By claiming that "generation" means "race", the millennialists completely miss the significance of the phrase "this generation" as used by Jesus in the Matthew 24:34, Mark 13:30, and Luke 21:32. This phrase concerns Israel's last days second-exodus-generation that was taking place in the first century. (Compare Numbers 32:1-15 with Hebrews 3:1-4:11)

to his deeds", does not refer to the second coming of Christ at the time of the judgment and resurrection?16 It is hard to imagine how anyone can seriously suggest that the coming of the Son of Man in the glory of his Father, with his angels, to judge all men, and to establish his kingdom, was fulfilled at either the transfiguration, the cross, the ascension, or Pentecost.

Furthermore, can the historical situation that surrounded these first century events account for the fulfillment of these eschatological elements found in Matthew 16? Commenting on the popular position that Matthew 16:27-28 was fulfilled at the transfiguration event only six days later, Russell says, "To suppose that it refers merely to the glorious manifestation of Jesus on the mount of transfiguration, though an hypothesis which has great names to support it, is   so palpably inadequate as an interpretation that is scarcely requires refutation."17 I completely agree, especially when we consider context.

And what about the idea that the AD70 coming of Christ in the judgment and destruction of Jerusalem was but a type or a foreshadowing of the *"real"* and yet-future-to-us second coming? 18 If all these eschatological elements - the Parousia, the judgment, resurrection, the establishment of the kingdom etc. - found their fulfillment in the first century; by what biblical authority do we look for another (greater) fulfillment thousands of years later? The fact is, such a "double fulfillment hermeneutic" should be seen for exactly what it is; a desperate attempt to maintain a futurist eschatology at all costs. Russell had this to say regarding this double fulfillment hermeneutic employed by Lang in the citations we quoted earlier: "His exegesis is so curious an illustration of the shifts to which the advocates of a double-sense theory of interpretation are compelled to resort."19 Again, I could not agree more.

We will now begin to demonstrate that Matthew 16:27-28 does in fact refer to

---

16. We simply mention this connection in passing and will develop it further below. For now, notice the connection between Matthew 16:27-28 Revelation 20:11-13 and Revelation 22:6-12 within the context of "the great white throne judgment". These parallels alone destroy all futurist views of the second coming.
17. James Stuart Russell, *The Parousia*, pp.29-30
18. For an exhaustive study demonstrating that the AD70 destruction of Jerusalem was not a "type or foreshadow" of the *"real"* end, I recommend Don K. Preston's book, *"AD70: A Shadow of the "Real" End"?* Don proves definitively that such an idea is both unbiblical and unwarranted.
19. James Stuart Russell, *The Parousia*, p.30

the second coming of Christ to consummate the salvation of all Israel through the establishment of his rule and reign (his kingdom) in fulfillment of the Old Testament scriptures. By doing so, we will by implication effectively refute the above futurist interpretations of Matthew 16:27-28, as well as the unbiblical doctrine of a future-to-us visible return of Jesus in a glorified flesh and bone body. As we continue our investigation, I believe you will be amazed by the clarity and consistency in which the scriptures in both Old and New Testaments plainly teach the doctrine of a *first century* second coming of Jesus Christ.

PART II

IDENTIFYING THE PRIMARY PROPHETIC SOURCES FOR MATTHEW 16:27-28

KEEPING IT IN CONTEXT

At this point it seems fitting to read again the words of James Stuart Russell….

"This passage alone contains so much important truth respecting the Parousia, that it may be said to cover the whole ground; and, rightly used, will be found to be a key to the true interpretation of the New Testament doctrine on this subject". 1

And here again is that passage….

> Matthew 16:27-28
> For the Son of Man is going to come in the glory of His Father with His angels, and will then repay every man according to his deeds. Truly I say to you, there are some of those who are standing here who will not taste death until they see the Son of Man coming in His kingdom.

This is where the eschatological rubber must hit the road. As we have shown above, the time element of the text, *"some of those who are standing here who will not taste death"* is all but universally agreed to refer to Jesus' contemporary generation. Therefore, if we can prove beyond doubt that verse 27 and 28 of Matthew 16 cannot be divided by thousands of years, and, that the prophecy itself does refer to the second coming event, then the second coming of Christ must have been fulfilled in the lifetime of Jesus' first disciples. To prove this is to falsify and refute all futurist schemes.

What will become obvious to the reader as we proceed, is that all futurist views 2 of Matthew 16:27-28 make two monumental exegetical blunders when seeking to interpret the text. First, they fail to interpret the text *within the framework of its Old Testament prophetic sources*. This is a lamentable oversight. When interpreting the words and prophesies of Jesus, we must always remember that….

> "…. Christ has become a servant to the circumcision on behalf of the truth of God *to confirm the promises given to the fathers…."* (Romans 15:8)

---

1. James Stuart Russell, *The Parousia*, p.32
2. By "futurist views" of Matthew 16:27-28, we mean any interpretation that places the "final and ultimate" fulfillment of the passage beyond AD70, more specifically, yet in our future.

After all, it was Jesus himself who said....

".... I was sent only to the lost sheep of the house of Israel." (Matthew 15:24)

We must therefore interpret the mission of the Master both in word and in deed through the filter of these truths. What this means is that the entire ministry of Jesus; whether through miracles, prophesies, or parables, must be understood first and foremost as the confirmation, yet redefinition, of the Old Testament promises made to Israel. In other words, the fulfillment of Matthew 16:27-28 would be the fulfillment of Old Testament prophecy, and make no mistake, those prophecies carried a specific framework and context in which they were   to be fulfilled. More on this momentarily.

Second, all futurist views of Matthew 16:27-28 fail to interpret the passage *within the narrative of its own immediate context.* This is doubly lamentable. Both these oversights (if they can be called that) have led to the bizarre futurist interpretations cited previously. Through a brief exegesis of Matthew 16:27-28, which will effectively establish the overall framework in which the passage should be interpreted. The understanding we gain here will be of much use to us later.

What cannot be overlooked is that the coming of the Son of Man in Matthew 16:27-28 is firmly placed within the context of "vindicatory judgment". In other words, the coming of Christ in his kingdom would be his coming to "repay every man" for shedding innocent blood. As Don Preston has well noted: "In Matthew 16:23f, Jesus foretold his own suffering, and that of his disciples. It is in the context of the prediction of that suffering that Jesus then says, "For the Son of Man will come in the glory of the Father." What this means is that the coming of verse 27-28 was to be Christ's coming *to vindicate his own suffering and that of his disciples."* 3 I could not agree more.

Preston goes on to point out that since according to Jesus in Matthew 23:29f, the vindication of "all the righteous blood shed upon the earth" would occur at

---

3.   Don K. Preston, *Can You Believe Jesus Said This?* (Ardmore, Oklahoma; JaDon Productions LLC, 2006), p.9. Preston also connects the coming of the Son of Man with the "glory of the Father" to emphasize both the time and nature of the second coming. This is a powerful point. See Preston's book, Like Father Like Son on Clouds of Glory for an exhaustive investigation of what it meant for Jesus to come in the "glory of the Father".

the judgment of Jerusalem in AD70, then the coming of Jesus to vindicate his own blood and the blood of his disciples in Matthew 16:27-28 must also have occurred in that generation. 4 Once again I completely agree. Furthermore, if we back up just a few more verses in Matthew 16, we can "double down" on Preston's position that this coming of Jesus was in fact his coming to avenge the blood of both himself and his disciples. More specifically, it was his coming in vindication to repay those who had "taken their stand against him" in fulfillment of Psalms 2.

In Matthew 16:13 Jesus began asking his disciples, "Who do people say that the Son of Man is?" In response, Peter says in verse 16, "You are the Christ, the Son of the living God". In my opinion, this is where the context of judgment and martyr vindication begins. Peter has just confessed that Jesus is the Lord's anointed King and Son of Psalm 2. 5 What is significant about this is that Psalm 2 prophesied the rejection of the Lord's anointed followed by his vindicatory enthronement and judgment over those who had gathered together against him. This is the prophetic source behind the context of judgment in Matthew 16. In other words, *it's the context behind the context.*

In verse 21 Jesus tells his disciples that "He must go to Jerusalem, and suffer many things from the elders and chief priests and scribes, and be killed, and be raised up on the third day". In the plainest of words, Jesus was letting them know that the *rulers of the land* were about to *take their stand against him*; Psalm 2 was about to be fulfilled. Likewise, when Jesus says in verse 24, "If anyone wishes to come after Me, he must deny himself, and take up his cross and follow Me"; he was telling his disciples how to "follow him" into Zion, that is, into his glory. Every man who would deny himself by "taking up his cross" (suffering with him 6) would find life in the kingdom. Every man who would not would be shattered in the day of his wrath. Either way, all would be "rewarded according to their works" at his coming in judgment.

---

4. Ibid. p.9 (a paraphrase of Preston's words)
5. It is significant that immediately following this allusion to Psalms 2, Jesus mentions the building of his church in Matthew 16:18. I can't help but see in this a reference to 2 Samuel 7:12-13 and the promise that the "Son of God" would build a house for the Lord, and the Lord would build a house for David. In Matthew 16 we see the church as both the house of David and House of the Lord being established in righteousness, in Zion.
6. Paul teaches the same thing in Romans 8:17-20 and 2 Timothy 2:12. Just as Jesus had to suffer to enter into his glory (Luke 24:26), so would his first century disciples (1 Peter 1:3-13).

Matthew 16:27-28 concerns neither Pentecost, the ascension, nor the transfiguration six days later; neither can these two verses be separated by several generations, never mind thousands of years. The coming of the Son of man in his kingdom was his coming to judge his enemies who had gathered together against him, to vindicate the sufferings of himself and his church, and to establish his reign as King in Mt. Zion. Psalms 2 prophesied the vindicatory second coming of Christ, which the Lord himself promised to accomplish within the lifetime of his first disciples.

Although Psalms 2 does play a significant role in properly interpreting Matthew 16:27-28, I see it as somewhat of a cameo in comparison to the other prophetic sources which lie behind this amazing passage. It is to those Old Testament prophesies that we now turn our investigation.

STATING THE ARGUMENT

Once again, we must always remember that in Matthew 16:27-28 Jesus was quoting and confirming, yet at the same time radically redefining, some of the most anticipated and significant Old Testament prophecies concerning the covenant-return of Yahweh to his people. But, before we cite the primary prophecies that Jesus was drawing from, allow me to state our argument which we will vindicate below.

-The prophetic source and background of Matthew 16:27-28 consists of four 1 Old Testament prophecies.

-But, those four Old Testament prophecies predicted the eschatological (last days) covenant-return (second coming) of Yahweh to Israel.

-Therefore, Matthew 16:27-28 prophesied the second coming of Christ as the covenant-return of Yahweh to Israel in fulfillment of these four Old Testament prophesies.

The four Old Testament prophesies that serve as the source and background for Matthew 16:27-28 are:

1.   Daniel 7:13-14
2.   Isaiah 59:17-21
3.   Isaiah 40:10-11
4.   Isaiah 62:10-12

So, to accomplish what we have set out to do - to establish the first century second coming of Christ - we must demonstrate definitively that all four texts are in fact the prophetic source of Matthew 16:27-28, and, that all four texts did in fact prophesy the second coming of Christ (the eschatological return of Yahweh) in fulfillment of the promises made to the fathers. I hope you're still with us, this is about to get very interesting.

---

1.   There are far more than four Old Testament prophecies that form the prophetic matrix of Matthew 16:27-28, Psalms 2 and Psalms 110 of course being one of them. These four are simply some of the more obvious and significant.

MATTHEW 16:27-28 = DANIEL 7:13-14

The first Old Testament prophecy that we will identify as a prophetic source of Matthew 16:27-28 is Daniel 7:13-14. Although there is much disagreement on the interpretation of this passage, we hope to demonstrate that most if not all of it has been completely unwarranted. Below are the two texts, one after another.

> Daniel 7:13-14
> "I kept looking in the night visions, and behold, with the clouds of heaven *One like a Son of Man was coming*... And *to Him was given dominion, glory and a kingdom*..."

> Matthew 16:27-28
> *"For the Son of Man is going to come* in the glory of His Father... Truly I say to you, there are some of those who are standing here who will not taste death until they see *the Son of Man coming in His kingdom.*"

Undeniably, Jesus is Daniel's "Son of man" whom Daniel saw coming with the clouds to receive His kingdom. In Matthew 16:27-28 Jesus quotes Daniel's prophecy, and promises that he, the Son of Man, will come (return) in the glory of his Father to establish His kingdom within the lifetime of His first century disciples. In other words, Jesus promised to fulfill Daniel's vision-prophecy within the lifetime of His contemporary generation. Now, in order to demonstrate beyond just a similarity of language that Daniel 7:13-14 was in fact a source for Jesus' prophecy, consider the following chart which takes into consideration a slightly larger context.

MATTHEW 16:27-28	DANIEL 7
Coming of the Son of Man (16:27)	Coming of the Son of Man (7:13)
In glory (16:27)	In glory (7:9,14)
With the angels (16:27)	Thousands upon thousands attending him (7:10)
To judge of every man according to their deeds (16:27)	Myriads upon myriads stood before Him, the books were opened (7:9-10,22,26)
To establish the kingdom (16:28)	To establish the kingdom (7:14,22)
Fulfilled in the lifetime of Jesus' first century disciples (16:28)	Fulfilled in the "last days" (Daniel 2:28f-parallel text) The last days were in the 1st century (Acts 2:15-17, Hebrews 1:1-2)

Based on these perfect parallels, consider the following argument:

-The coming of the Son of Man in Daniel 7 = the coming of the Son of Man in Matthew 16:27-28.
-But, the coming of the Son of Man in Daniel 7 refers to the second coming of Christ.
-Therefore, the coming of the Son of Man in Matthew 16:27-28 refers to the second coming of Christ in fulfillment of Daniel 7:13-14.

Assuming this is true, consider what follows:

-The coming of the Son of Man in Matthew 16:27-28 refers to the second coming of Christ in fulfillment of Daniel 7:13-14.
-But, the second coming of Christ in Matthew 16:27-28 was fulfilled in the lifetime of the first century disciples. (Matthew 16:28)
-Therefore, the second coming of Christ in fulfillment of Daniel 7:13-14 took place in the lifetime of the first century disciples. 1

Yet, some will waive their hands and blow their whistles at this argument based on their rejection of Daniel 7:13-14 as a "second coming passage"; insisting that Daniel's Son of Man "coming on the clouds of heaven" finds fulfillment at the ascension of Jesus. For example, N.T. Wright says, "Daniel 7 conceives the scene from the perspective of heaven, not earth. The "son of man" figure "comes" to the Ancient of Days. He comes *from* earth *to* heaven, vindicated after suffering."2 However, as we shall see, this application of Jesus' coming in Daniel's prophecy only serves to further demonstrate the desperation of interpreters to maintain their belief in a future-to-us bodily return of Jesus. The futurist failure to miss the overall vindicatory judgment context of Matthew 16 is repeated once again in Daniel 7.

---

1. Despite the claims of some "former preterists", the undeniable fact that Jesus and the writers of the New Testament consistently applied the prophesies of Daniel to the first century Parousia event, proves beyond doubt that those very prophesies - specifically chapters 2,7,9,12 - were in factMessianic.
2. N.T. Wright, *Jesus And The Victory of God*, (Minneapolis; Fortress Press, 1996), p.361. Wright is correct to see the coming of the Son of Man in Daniel 7 as vindicatory, yet clearly wrong based on the context to identify the ascension event as its fulfillment. Daniel 7 is uniquely the coming of the Son of Man in vindication of the saints following a three and a half year persecution by the "little horn". This was clearly not the historical context of the ascension of Jesus.

Notice that in Daniel's vision, the One like a Son of Man receives a kingdom following the judgment of a "little horn".

> Daniel 7:8-10,13
> While I was contemplating the horns, behold, *another horn, a little one, came up among them...* this horn possessed eyes like the eyes of a man and a mouth uttering great boasts. I kept looking until thrones were set up, and *the Ancient of Days took His seat....* Thousands upon thousands were attending Him, and myriads upon myriads were standing before Him; *the court sat, and the books were opened.* Then I kept looking because of the sound of the boastful words which the horn was speaking; I kept looking until *the beast was slain, and its body was destroyed and given to the burning fire.....* I kept looking in the night visions, and behold, *with the clouds of heaven One like a Son of Man was coming,* and He came up to the Ancient of Days and was presented before Him....

As the vision continues it is further explained. Daniel is told that the little horn wages war against the saints and overpowers them for a "time, times and half a time" (three and a half years).

> Daniel 7:21,25
> I kept looking, and *that horn was waging war with the saints and overpowering them.... He will speak out against the Most High and wear down the saints of the Highest One,* and he will intend to make alterations in times and in law; and *they will be given into his hand for a time, times, and half a time.*

As God's vehicle of vengeance, the little horn was empowered to wage war on Israel ("the saints" at the time of Daniel's writing) for their persecution of his church. When that punishment was accomplished, the Ancient of Days came 3 and the dominion which the little horn wielded was removed. Thus, the church was avenged, and the time came for the saints (the remnant) to receive the dominion of the kingdom.

---

3. The coming of the Ancient of Days is verse 22 represents the coming of the Son in the "glory of the Father" (Matthew 16:27). The coming of the Son of Man would be the revelation of Christ as the Ancient of Days. In John 14:23 Jesus said that both He and the Father would "come". Thus, the picture we have in Daniel 7 is the Son approaching the Father (post-Parousia) to receive the kingdom in all its fullness, yet at the same time, the Son is being revealed as "One with the Father". (Also see Titus 2:13.)

Daniel 7:22,26-27

".... *the Ancient of Days came* and judgment was passed in favor of the saints of the Highest One, and *the time arrived when the saints took possession of the kingdom.... But the court will sit for judgment and his dominion will be taken away,* annihilated and destroyed forever.... Then *the sovereignty, the dominion and the greatness of all the kingdoms under the whole heaven will be given to the people of the saints of the Highest One...."*

Therefore, according to the context of Daniel 7, the coming of the Son of Man would be in both judgment and vindication resulting in the establishment of   the kingdom. So, if the coming of the Son of Man in Daniel 7 refers to Christ's ascension, the following questions need to be asked. Had a "little horn" 4 waged war against the saints 5 for a time, times and half a time (three and a half years) prior to the ascension? Or, had the saints 6 fully received the kingdom as their reward and vindication for their sufferings at or prior to that event? The obvious answer to both these questions is no, yet this is precisely the context for the coming of the Son of Man in Daniel 7 as well as Matthew 16:27-28. 7 Clearly, Daniel 7 did not find fulfillment at or before the ascension of Jesus in AD30.

---

4.   Regardless of whether the identity of the little horn was Roman or Jewish, the point remains the same. The coming of the Son of Man in Daniel 7 takes place *after a three and a half year persecution*, not before. It is the opinion of the author that the little horn should be identified as a Jewish persecutor.

5.   It is also the opinion of the author that the "saints" (holy ones) that are persecuted by the little horn for a time, times, and half a time (three and a half years) are also Jewish, that is, they are Old Covenant Israel. This agrees perfectly with Daniel 12, where a "time of distress" comes upon Daniel's "holy people" (12:1), that lasts for a "time, times, and a half a time", resulting in the "shattering of the power of the holy people"; Old Covenant Israel. (12:7).

6.   The "saints' who receive the kingdom at the coming of the Son of Man are the righteous remnant of Old Covenant Israel who had been persecuted by their own countrymen, the Jews.

7.   The pattern of persecution-judgment-vindication is powerfully present in both Matthew and Daniel, yet the emphasis of the texts is somewhat different. In Matthew 16 we see a Jewish persecution of the church, followed by the judgment of the persecutors at the coming of the Son of Man bringing vindication to the saints. In Daniel 7 we see a persecution of the Jews by the *Zealot regime within Jerusalem* as part of God's judgment for their persecution of his church. At the coming of the Son of Man both the persecutor and the persecuted (who were both Jewish entities) were judged and destroyed, bringing vindication to the saints, the righteous remnant.

Therefore, the coming of the Son of Man in Daniel 7:13-14 could not possibly have been fulfilled through that event. What this means is that there is no biblical reason whatsoever to reject Matthew 16:27-28 as a second coming prophecy based on the argument that the coming of the Son of Man in Daniel 7:13-14 was fulfilled at the ascension. N.T. Wright is a brilliant scholar in many ways and I admire much of his work, yet concerning the prophetic scope and fulfillment of Daniel 7, Wright is not right, Wright is wrong.

A CLOSER LOOK AT DANIEL 7
TIME, TIMES AND A HALF A TIME

A closer look at the larger context of Daniel 7 will reveal the precise biblical timeframe for the fulfillment of the coming of the Son of Man on the clouds of heaven. There are two significant events found in Daniel 7 that are "keys" to rightly understanding the prophecy. These events are:

1. Time, times and half a time
2. When the saints took possession of the kingdom.

Now, since these two events are synchronous with the coming of the Son of Man, if we establish the *time* of these events, we will have established the *time* of his coming. Let's begin with event #1. The parallel chart below reveals that Daniel's time, times and half a time, and John's forty-two months refer to the same persecution, of the same people, at the *same time*.

DANIEL 7	REVELATION 13
Beasts coming up from the sea (7:3)	A beast coming up out of the sea (13:1)
The beast had 10 horns (7:7)	The beast had 10 horns (13:1)
Spoke boastful words against the Most High (7:11,20,25)	Spoke arrogant words and blasphemies against God (13:5-6)
Made war with the saints and overpowered them, for a time, times and half a time (7:21,25)	Made war with the saints and overcome them, for forty-two months (13:5-7)

Clearly, Daniel's time, times and half a time, and John's forty-two months prophesied the same events. Yet, undeniably, John's forty-two months in Revelation 13 were not fulfilled at the ascension of Jesus in AD30. In fact, since John was seeing things that were to "soon take place,"1 John's forty-two months could not have been fulfilled prior to the time that John wrote Revelation. 2 This proves that Daniel's time, times, and a half a time must have been fulfilled after John wrote Revelation, not at the ascension. But that's not all. The next chart demonstrates that the time, times and half a time in Daniel 7 also refers

---

1. Revelation 1:1, 22:6
2. This author takes the position that Revelation was written prior to the beginning of the Jewish-Roman war in 66AD. See Kenneth Gentry's *"The Days of Vengeance"* and Don K. Preston's *"Who Is This Babylon"* for powerful evidence in support of the early dating of Revelation.

to the *same period of persecution* that was to come upon Daniel's holy people as prophesied in Daniel 12. Notice....

DANIEL 7	DANIEL 12
The saints worn down and overpowered (7:21,25)	A time of great distress, the power of the holy people completely shattered (12:1,7)
Time, times and half a time (7:25)	Time, times and half a time (12:7)
Time of the judgment and resurrection (7:9-10,22-27)	Time of the judgment and resurrection (12:1-3,7,13)
Concerned the last days (Daniel 2:28 - parallel prophecy)	Concerned the time of the end (12:4,9,13)

These parallels are important when we come to the gospels. When Jesus quoted Daniel 12:1 in Matthew 24:21, he was clearly identifying Daniel's "time of distress" (which lasted for a time, times, and half a time 3) as the "great tribulation".

> "And *there will be a time of distress such as never occurred since there was a nation,* until that time...." (Daniel 12:1)

> "For then *there will be a great tribulation, such as has not occurred since the beginning of the world* until now, nor ever will". (Matthew 24:21)

Luke's account sharpens the edge of Jesus' words in Matthew by interpreting the great tribulation *to be* the "days of vengeance" (Luke 21:22) and time of "great distress" upon Israel, which would be accomplished when Jerusalem was surrounded by the armies of Rome in the first century.

> "But *when you see Jerusalem surrounded by armies,* then recognize that her desolation is near.... because *these are days of vengeance,* so that all things which are written will be fulfilled.... for *there will be great distress upon the land and wrath to this people.* (Luke 21:20,22-23)

---

3. The connection between Israel's "time of distress", the "time, times and a half a time", and the "shattering of the power of the holy people" in Daniel 12 should not be missed. Israel would suffer severe distress for three and a half years resulting in the shattering of their power. Jesus identifies this as Israel's first century great tribulation which culminated with the fall of Jerusalem in AD70.

Jesus' application of Daniel 12 in both Matthew 24 and Luke 21 literally demands that Daniel's time, times and half be understood as the first century great tribulation, the siege of Jerusalem by Rome between AD66-70. That siege culminated in Jerusalem's utter destruction and the "shattering 4 of the power of the holy people", that is, the removal of the Old Covenant world.

With this established, consider the following argument:
-The time, times and a half a time in Daniel 7 = the time, times and half a time in Daniel 12.

-But, the time, times and a half a time in Daniel 12 was the great tribulation/days of vengeance, when Jerusalem was besieged and destroyed between AD66-70.

-Therefore, the time, times and half a time in Daniel 7 was the great tribulation/days of vengeance, when Jerusalem was besieged and destroyed between AD66-70.

This being true, consider what follows:
-The time, times, and half a time in Daniel 7 was the great tribulation/days of vengeance, when Jerusalem was besieged and destroyed between AD66-70.

-But, the coming of the Son of Man on the clouds of heaven in Daniel 7 takes place at the time, times and a half a time - the siege and destruction of Jerusalem between AD66-70.

-Therefore, the coming of the Son of Man on the clouds of heaven in Daniel 7:13-14 takes place at the siege and destruction of Jerusalem between AD66-70.

And, as inspired confirmation of the above arguments, this is precisely the *time and context* in which Jesus placed his "coming on the clouds" in fulfillment of Daniel 7:13.

---

4. The Hebrew word translated as "shattering" in Daniel 12:7 is "naphats". The same word is used in Psalms 2:9 as the "shattering like earthenware" of those who would persist in standing against the Lord and his Anointed. Thus, Daniel 12, a prophetic source of Matthew 16:27-28 is thematically connected to Psalms 2, the prophetic source for the larger context of Matthew 16. Therefore, the judgment prophesied in Psalms 2 was the shattering of Israel's power in Daniel 12. Both Psalms 2 and Daniel 12 were fulfilled at the coming of the Son of Man in Matthew 16:27-28 in the first century.

Luke 21:20,22,27,32

But *when you see Jerusalem surrounded by armies,* then recognize that her desolation is near.... because *these are days of vengeance,* so that all things which are written will be fulfilled.... *Then they will see the Son of Man coming in a cloud* with power and great glory.... Truly I say to you, *this generation will not pass away until all things take place.*

We conclude that the coming of the Son of Man following the time, times and half a time in Daniel 7, prophesied the second coming of Christ and was fulfilled at the fall of Jerusalem in AD70. Therefore, in fulfillment of Daniel 7, Matthew 16:27-28 prophesied the second coming of Christ to bring both judgment and salvation to Israel (Luke 21:28) and was accomplished at the fall of Jerusalem in AD70, within the lifetime of Jesus' contemporary disciples.

WHEN THE SAINTS TOOK
POSSESSION OF THE KINGDOM

We will now establish the biblical timeframe for the second event found in Daniel 7, *"when the saints took possession of the kingdom"*. As we shall see, the context of Daniel 7 as well as it's parallel passages make it abundantly clear that the saints did not take possession of the kingdom at the ascension of Jesus in 30AD; but rather, some forty years later at the fall of Jerusalem in AD70. Below is the passage from Daniel 7 once again.

> Daniel 7:13,18,21-22
> I kept looking in the night visions, and behold, *with the clouds of heaven One like a Son of Man was coming,* and He came up to the Ancient of Days and was presented before Him…. But *the saints of the Highest One will receive the kingdom and possess the kingdom* forever, for all ages to come….
> I kept looking, and *that horn was waging war with the saints and overpowering them until the Ancient of Days came* and judgment was passed in favor of the saints of the Highest One, and *the time arrived when the saints took possession of the kingdom.*

While it is true that the saints were on some level experiencing the kingdom (the rule and reign of God) beginning the day of Pentecost as a result of the ascension of Jesus, 1 this most assuredly did not fulfill what Daniel predicted. As Sam Dawson points out concerning Daniel 7; "the saints in this conflict will both *receive* the kingdom and *possess* the kingdom, but at two different times. It's not until God sits for judgment that the saints *take possession* of the kingdom." 2 I tend to agree with Sam, this is precisely the picture and progression that we see in several of Jesus' parables.

Also, recall that the specific relationship between "kingdom and saints" in Daniel 7 (and Matthew 16:27-28) is the possession of the kingdom *as the reward* for their sufferings. In other words, the saints possess the kingdom *as the result of* their persecution and *as vindication of it*, not prior to it. Notice verses 21 and 22 in particular.

---

1. Acts 2:29-39, Romans 14:17, Colossians 1:13, Hebrews 12:28, Revelation 1:6,9
2. Samuel G. Dawson, *Revelation Realized Martyr Vindication from Genesis to Revelation,* (Bowie, Texas; SGD Press, 2016), p.170

"I kept looking, and *that horn was waging war with the saints and overpowering them until the Ancient of Days came* and judgment was passed in favor of the saints of the Highest One, *and the time arrived when the saints took possession of the kingdom"*.

A brief investigation of just two of the parables of Jesus will help us to better understand this portion of Daniel's prophecy. In Matthew 25, the kingdom is not "possessed" when the slaves of the Master are entrusted with his goods (his rule and dominion) *at the beginning of his journey.* 3 This part of the parable corresponds to the *initiation of the kingdom,* when he "ascended on high" and "gave gifts to men." 4 Rather, the saints take possession of the kingdom (entering the joy of their Master) when the Master *returns from his journey* to "settle accounts" with the slaves. 5 This clearly corresponds to the Parousia, the second coming of Christ. Those who had been faithful with the Master's goods (had expanded his rule and dominion), would then *take possession of them,* that is, they would inherit the kingdom of God. 6

Similarly, the time when the saints took possession of the kingdom did not take place when the Noblemen in Luke 19 *went to the distant country* to receive a kingdom". 7 This part of the parable points again to the coronation of Christ at his ascension in fulfillment of Psalms 2 and Psalms 110. Rather, it was at the *return of that Noblemen* that his servants received their reward (possession of the kingdom), while judgment was meted out to those who "did not want him to reign over them." 8 Once again, an obvious allusion to the Parousia of Christ. To understand these parables of Jesus is to understand this prophecy of Daniel, and vice-versa.

In conclusion, the time when the saints took possession of the kingdom in Daniel 7 is set firmly within the context and framework of the judgment of the enemies of Christ, and the vindication of his faithful servants. This effectively eliminates the ascension of Jesus in AD30 as a plausible biblical option for the fulfillment of the coming of the Son of Man in Daniel 7:13-14 and by implication, Matthew

---

3.   Matthew 25:14
4.   Ephesians 4:8
5.   Matthew 25:19-23
6.   Matthew 25:34
7.   Luke 19:12
8.   Luke 19:14,27. Significantly, both Matthew 25 and Luke 19 also contain the same pattern of persecution-judgment-vindication in the context of the coming of the Lord as does Daniel 7 and Matthew 16.

16:27-28. It seems to me that the only historical event of the first century which meets the biblical criteria of both judgment and vindication in the context of the kingdom, is the fall of Jerusalem in AD70; which accomplished both the judgment of the Jewish nation, and the vindication of the people of God. As we shall see, this is precisely what Jesus predicted in one of his most provocative parables.

ISRAEL THE LORD'S VINEYARD

In Matthew 21, Jesus told a parable in which he specifically identified *the time* that the saints would possess the kingdom in fulfillment of Daniel 7, as the judgment of the Jews and the removal of their Old Covenant kingdom in AD70. But before we get there, notice the absolute perfect parallel between Matthew 21:43 and Daniel 7:22.

> "... *the kingdom of God will be* taken away from you and *given to a people...*"
> (Matthew 21:43)

> "... the time arrived when *the saints took possession of the kingdom*"
> (Daniel 7:22)

Jesus was communicating in the clearest most emphatic way possible, that what his followers were soon to receive would be in fulfillment of what Daniel had long ago predicted. Notice the larger context of the parable of the vineyard.

> Matthew 21:33-44
> Listen to another parable. *There was a landowner who planted a vineyard* 1 and put a wall around it and dug a winepress in it, and built a tower, and rented it out to vine-growers and went on a journey. When the harvest time approached, he sent his slaves to the vine-growers to receive his produce. The vine-growers took his slaves and beat one, and killed another, and stoned a third. Again, he sent another group of slaves larger than the first; and they did the same thing to them. But afterward he sent his son .... They took him, and threw him out of the vineyard and killed him. Therefore, when the owner of the vineyard comes, what will he do to those vine-growers? They said to Him, *He will bring those wretches to a wretched end, and will rent out the vineyard to other vine-growers* who will pay him the proceeds at the proper seasons. Therefore, I say to you, *the kingdom of God will be taken away from you and given to a people, producing the fruit of it.* 2 And he who falls on this stone

---

1. Isaiah 5 and the parable of the vineyard of the Lord of Hosts (5:7) lies behind this parable of Jesus. First century Old Covenant Israel was the Lord's unfruitful vineyard who was about to be uprooted and destroyed.
2. This prophecy of the "kingdom being taken" from Israel would also be in fulfillment of Genesis 49:10. When Shiloh arrived in Israel's last days, the "scepter" (the authority) would depart from Judah as a covenant nation. Significantly, Israel's last days had arrived when Jesus spoke this prophecy. (Hebrews 1:1-2).

will be broken to pieces; but on whomever it falls, it will scatter him like dust."3

Due to a long and unfruitful reign, the Old Covenant kingdom (expressed as Judaism) would be taken from ethnic Israel and given (in its New Covenant expression) to another people.4 We should also point out the fact that within this parable we find the pattern of persecution-judgment-vindication that we have seen so often before. The implication is simple. The kingdom would be taken from Judah as judgment for their murder of the Son and his saints; while the kingdom given to others as their reward and vindication for their suffering.5 There can be no doubt whatsoever that this good news/bad news parable pointed no further than the conflagration of Jerusalem and the destruction of that wicked and sinful generation 6 in AD70.7 As a matter of fact, Matthew even records that the rulers of Jerusalem understood it in just this way.

---

3. This imagery of a stone breaking and scattering like dust is an allusion back to Daniel 2:34-35,44. In Israel's last days, (Daniel 2:28) the stone "cut without hands" (the kingdom of God) would crush and put an end to the pagan dominions that had ruled over the righteous of Israel. Here, Jesus identifies Israel of his day as a pagan enemy of Yahweh - Daniel's 4th beast - that would be crushed at the full arrival and manifestation of the kingdom. It is interesting to note that this crushing of God's enemies by the corner stone of the new temple, is placed in the context of the destruction of the nation. Thus, those who would reject their Messiah would be crushed by stones from both earthly and spiritual temples.

4. Not only is Matthew 21:43 a direct allusion to Daniel 7:22, but also to Isaiah 65:1-15; where following the judgment and destruction of the rebellious house of Israel, the righteous remnant becomes a new people with a new name, established as a new creation. This is undoubtedly the time when the saints *possess* the kingdom.

5. The fact that Jesus placed the judgment to avenge the blood of all the righteous shed since the foundation of the world in his generation, (Luke 11:50, Matthew 23:23:31f) is undeniable proof that the saints received the kingdom in fulfillment of Matthew 21:33f and Daniel 7 at the fall of Jerusalem in AD70 (Luke 21:20-32), when the blood of Christ and his followers was to be avenged.

6. Mark 8:38-9:1

7. Jesus' parable in Matthew 21 also parallels perfectly with Daniel 12. The removal of the kingdom from Judah (Matthew 21:43), was the shattering of the power (covenant dominion) of the holy people (Daniel 12:7). This was accomplished through Jerusalem's demise in AD70 following her time of distress for a time, times, and half a time.

Matthew 21:45
"When the chief priests and the Pharisees heard His parables, *they understood that He was speaking about them*".

According to their own admission, these chief priests and Pharisees to whom Jesus spoke considered themselves to be, at the very least, "the builders" who were presently rejecting the cornerstone of the new temple.8 Only several months later, those same men were warned by Peter and John that unless they would fall on that Stone and be broken, the Stone that "they the builders" had rejected, would fall upon them and "grind them to powder".9

Acts 4:10-12
Let it be known to all of you and to all the people of Israel, that by the name of *Jesus Christ the Nazarene, whom you crucified,* whom God raised from the dead - by this name this man stands here before you in good health. *He is the stone which was rejected by you, the builders,* but which became the chief cornerstone. And there is salvation in no one else; for there is no other name under heaven that has been given among   men by which we must be saved." 10

Thus, both Jesus and Peter identified the rulers of Israel in their day as the builders of Psalms 118, who had rejected and crucified their Messiah. Furthermore, Jesus identified the judgment for that rejection as his avenging the murder of his saints, that is, martyr vindication. Therefore, the judgment   of those builders and the removal of their kingdom in the parable of the vineyard, must have taken place at the destruction of Jerusalem in AD70, when God would avenge all the righteous blood shed upon the earth.11

But remember, the removal of the kingdom from the Jews was to take place when that kingdom (in its New Covenant form) was given to another people (the church). Therefore, the time when the saints took possession of the kingdom was when Old Covenant Israel was judged and destroyed, and the rule and authority which they had possessed was taken from them. Once again, this did

---

8.   See comments above (#3) concerning the rejected stone in this context.
9.   Matthew 21:44 (this specific phrase is from the KJV).
10. Peter's call to salvation here harkens back to his warning of the Day of the Lord that was coming upon his generation from which they needed to be saved (Acts 2:17-21,40). This in turn points back to the message of John the Baptist who asked Israel of his day, "who warned you to flee from the wrath *to come*"? (Matthew 3:7) (More literally, *"about to come"*, from the Greek word "mello")
11. Matthew 23:29f, Luke 11:49f

not take place at the ascension of Jesus, but at the end of the Old Covenant age in AD70.

The following chart demonstrates that several of the major constituent elements found in Daniel 7 are also found in Matthew 21. This confirms again that these two passages speak of *same time events;* when the saints took possession of the kingdom at the coming of the Son of Man.

DANIEL 7	MATTHEW 21
Coming of the Son of Man/ Ancient of Days (7:13,22)	Coming of the Owner of the vineyard (21:40)
Persecutors of the saints judged, and the saints vindicated (7:21-27)	Persecutors of the saints judged, and the saints vindicated (21:35-43)
Saints receive the kingdom (7:18,22,27)	Saints receive the kingdom (21:43)

Clearly, both passages refer to the persecution of the saints, the judgment of their persecutors, and time when the saints took possession of the kingdom as vindication for their suffering. Yet in Matthew 21, the saints possess the kingdom at the judgment of Jerusalem in AD70. To drive this point home further, notice that these same constituent elements are also found in Luke's version of Jesus' Olivet discourse, which Jesus promised would be fulfilled in the lifetime of his contemporary generation.

DANIEL 7	MATTHEW 21	LUKE 21
Coming of the Son of Man on the clouds of heaven (7:13)	Coming of the owner of the vineyard (21:40)	Coming of the Son of Man on the clouds of heaven (21:27)
Persecutors of the saints judged and the saints vindicated (7:21-27)	Persecutors of the saints judged and the saints vindicated in Jerusalem's destruction in AD70. (21:35-43)	Persecutors of the saints judged and the saints vindicated in Jerusalem's destruction in AD70 (21:12-28)
Saints receive the kingdom when those who persecuted the saints were judged (7:18,22,27)	Saints receive the kingdom when those who persecuted the saints (Judah) were judged (21:35-45)	Saints receive the kingdom at the judgment of Jerusalem and Judah in AD70. (21:20-24,31)
Fulfilled in the "last days" (Daniel 2:28-parallel text) 1st century-Hebrews 1:1-2	Fulfilled at the Judgment of Jerusalem in AD70 (21:41-43)	All these things fulfilled in Jesus' generation (21:32)

Based on these perfect parallels, consider the following argument:

-The saints possessing the kingdom in Daniel 7 = the saints possessing the kingdom in Matthew 21 and Luke 21.

-But in Matthew 21 and Luke 21, the saints would take possession of the kingdom at the judgment of Jerusalem in AD70.

-*Therefore, the saints took possession of the kingdom in fulfillment of Daniel 7, at the judgment of Jerusalem in AD70.*

By comparing the key constituent elements as well as the overall framework of martyr vindication found in Daniel 7, Matthew 21 and Luke 21, we have definitively placed the time when the saints possessed the kingdom at the fall of Jerusalem and the end of the Old Covenant age in AD70. But, since the saints took possession of the kingdom at the coming of the Son of Man in Daniel 7, then the coming of the Son of Man in Matthew 16:27-28, in fulfillment of Daniel 7, must have been accomplished at the fall of Jerusalem and the end of the Old Covenant age in AD70.

REMOVING WHAT CAN BE SHAKEN

Let's look at one more passage which also clearly establishes the *time* when the "saints took possession of the kingdom" in fulfillment of Daniel 7, and by implication, Matthew 16:27-28. Once again, the biblical evidence powerfully points to the removal of the Old Covenant world in AD70.

> Hebrews 12:22,26-28 (NKJV)
> *"But you have come to Mount Zion....* Whose voice then shook the earth; but now He has promised, saying, "Yet once more, I shake not only the earth, but also heaven". 1 Now *this, "Yet once more" indicates the removal of those things that are being shaken,* as of things that are made, *that the things which cannot be shaken may remain.* Therefore, *since we are receiving a kingdom which cannot be shaken..."*

This Hebrews passage is extremely important as it relates to Daniel 7. Notice that the phrases "since we are *receiving* a kingdom" and "a kingdom which *cannot be shaken*", are both drawn directly from Daniel 7:18.2 Below are the parallel passages...

> "Therefore, since *we are receiving a kingdom which cannot be shaken..."* (Hebrews 12:28)

> *"But the saints of the Most High shall receive the kingdom,* and possess the kingdom forever, *even forever and ever"* (Daniel 7:18-NKJV)

This means that the church was the "saints of the Most High" that was at that time (62-63AD) in the process of receiving the everlasting kingdom, in fulfillment of Daniel 7. But, the context of Hebrews 12 is the removal of the Old

---

1. Hebrews 12:26 is a direct quotation of Haggai 2:6. The following is a quote from p.67 in my book, *"The Transition Between Two Covenants"*, which expresses the significance of the connection. "In Haggai chapter 2, the "shaking of heaven and earth" referred to the typological restoration of Israel from Babylonian captivity, climaxing in the beautification of the temple by Herod the Great. However, the writer of the book of Hebrews interprets this shaking of heaven and earth to refer to the *final* (once more) shaking and removing of the Old Covenant world system, and the final restoration of Israel through the establishment of the New Covenant order."

2. Hebrews 12:28 also points us back to Jesus' prophecy in Matthew 21:43. Jesus was emphatic that the remnant-saints (the other nation/people) would possess the Kingdom when national Israel was judged in AD70.

Covenant kingdom (Judaism), and the full arrival of the unshakable New Covenant world.3 Therefore, the saints were receiving the kingdom in fulfillment of Daniel 7 through the removal of the Jewish world in the first century. When Judaism had been fulfilled and fully removed, the saints took full possession of the kingdom.

To summarize, consider the following argument:
-The saints would take possession of the kingdom at the coming of the Son of Man (Daniel 7:13-22).

-But the saints would take possession of the kingdom at the removal of Judaism and the full arrival of the New Covenant world in AD70. (Hebrews 12:22-28).

-Therefore, saints took possession of the kingdom at the coming of the Son of Man to remove Old Covenant Judaism and establish the New Covenant world in AD70, in fulfillment of Daniel 7.

In conclusion, we have repeatedly shown that the persecution of the saints, the judgment of their persecutors, and the time when the saints took possession of the kingdom; form the framework and context for the coming of the Son of Man in both Daniel 7:13-14 and Matthew 16:27-28. We have also shown that each of these eschatological themes are *temporally interconnected* to the judgment of Jerusalem in AD70. This means the coming of the Son of Man in both Daniel 7 and Matthew 16:27-28 must have been fulfilled at the judgment of Jerusalem in AD70.

---

3. 2 Corinthians 3 is also a parallel text of Hebrews 12 in that it teaches a first century "covenant transition".

DANIEL 7 & REVELATION 19-20

What strikes me as peculiar is that many students of the bible, commentators included, not only fail to interpret Daniel 7 in its immediate context or through the prophesies and parables of Jesus, but *through its apostolic application in the book of Revelation*. We will now show conclusively that the coming of the Son of Man in Daniel 7 prophesied the first century second coming of Christ, in fulfillment of the Apocalypse, at the destruction of Jerusalem in AD70. Please examine carefully the following comparative chart:

DANIEL 7	REVELATION 19-20
The coming of the Son of Man in judgment (7:9,13,22,26)	The coming of Christ in judgment (19:11-13, 20:12-13)
Thousands upon thousands were attending him (7:10)	The armies which are in heaven… were following Him (19:14)
Myriads upon myriads stood before Him (7:10)	The dead, the great and the small standing before him (20:12)
Sat on the throne, the books were opened (7:9-10)	Sat on the throne, the books were opened (20:11-13)
The kingdom established, the saints receive/possess the kingdom (7:14,18,22,27)	The kingdom established, the saints receive/possess the kingdom (19:14-16, 20:4-6)
Fulfilled in the "last days" (Daniel 2:28f - parallel prophecy) 1st century - Hebrews 1:1-2	Fulfillment was "soon/near" in the first century (1:1-3, 22:6-7,10-12)

Based on these perfect parallels, consider the following argument:

-The coming of the Son of Man in Daniel 7 = the coming of Christ as King of Kings and Lord of Lords in Revelation 19-20.
-But the coming of Christ as King of Kings and Lord of Lords in Revelation 19-20 refers to Christ's second coming.
-Therefore, the coming of the Son of Man in Daniel 7 prophesied the second coming of Christ in fulfillment of Revelation 19-20.

These are impressive parallels with far reaching implications. Regardless of their millennial position, futurists are agreed, and rightly so, that the white- horse-coming of Christ followed by the armies of heaven in Revelation 19, refers to his second and final coming. After all, the coming of Christ in Revelation 19 is to execute the judgment of the dead in Revelation 20; when the books are opened at the time of the resurrection. But, since this judgment - coming of Christ in Revelation 19-20 is the coming of the Son of Man in Daniel 7, then

43

undeniably, the coming of the Son of Man in Daniel 7 must refer to the second coming of Christ.

Furthermore, as we have already demonstrated, the overarching theme and framework of Daniel 7 (as well as Matthew 16:27-28) is persecution-judgment-vindication. The Son of Man comes in judgment of the persecutors, and to vindicate the saints who were suffering. This is precisely the framework we find in the context of Revelation 19-21 as well. Christ comes in judgment against Babylon 1 to "avenge the blood of his bond-servants, 2 and to reward (vindicate) the saints at the wedding. 3 Daniel saw a last-days vision 4 of the restoration of Israel and the subjugation of their enemies at the coming of the Lord. John, living in Israel's last days 5 saw the exact same thing; only John was told, "Do not seal up the words of the prophecy of this book, *for the time is near.*" 6 Based on the evidence above, consider the following argument:

-The coming of the Son of Man in Daniel 7:13-14 = the second coming of Christ in Revelation 19-20.
-But the coming of the Son of Man in Daniel 7:13-14 = the coming of the Son of Man in Matthew 16:27-28.
-Therefore, the coming of the Son of Man in Matthew 16:27-28 prophesied the second coming of Christ in fulfillment of Revelation 19-20.

This being true, consider what *must* also be true:
-The coming of the Son of Man in Matthew 16:27-28 = the second coming of Christ in Daniel 7 and Revelation 19-20.
-But in Matthew 16:28, Jesus undeniably placed *the time* of his coming within the lifetime of his first century disciples.
-Therefore, the second coming of Christ in Matthew 16:27-28 must have taken place within the lifetime of his first century disciples, in fulfillment of Daniel 7 and Revelation 19-20.

---

1. For the most convincing and scholarly work available on the identity of Babylon of Revelation as Old Covenant Jerusalem, see Don K. Preston's book, *"Who Is This Babylon"*.
2. Revelation 19:2
3. Revelation 19:9
4. Daniel 2:28f (the vison in Daniel 2 is parallel to his vision in chapter 7)
5. Acts 2:15-17, Hebrews 1:1-2. Those days were the last days of the Old Covenant age (Hebrews 9:26)
6. Revelation 22:10. In contrast, Daniel who was told to "seal the book until the time of the end" (12:4 ESV).

The following chart illustrates the validity of the above arguments.

DANIEL 7	MATTHEW 16:27-28	REVELATION 19-20
The coming of the Son of Man in judgment (7:13,22)	The coming of the Son of Man in judgment (16:27)	The coming of Jesus in judgment (19:11-13, 20:12-13)
Coming in glory, throne ablaze with flames (7:9,14)	Coming in the glory of His Father (16:27)	His eyes a flame of fire, diadems on his head (19:12)
Thousands upon thousands attending him (7:10)	With his angels (16:27)	Armies in heaven were following him (19:14)
Myriads upon myriads stood before Him, the books were opened (7:10)	Judgment of every man according to their deeds (16:27)	The dead small and great were judged according to their deeds, the books were opened (20:12)
To establish the kingdom (7:14,22,27)	To establish the kingdom (16:28)	To establish the kingdom (19:14-16)
Fulfilled in the "last days" (Daniel 2:28 - parallel prophecy) 1st century-Hebrews 1:1-2	Fulfilled in the lifetime of Jesus' first century disciples (16:28)	Fulfillment was "soon/near in the first century (1:1-3, 22:6-7,10-12)

In conclusion, Daniel 7:13-14 prophesied the second coming of Christ and served as an Old Testament source for the coming of the Son of Man in Matthew 16:27-28. Therefore, the coming of the Son of Man in Matthew 16:27-28 prophesied the second coming of Christ and was accomplished in the lifetime of the first century generation at the judgment of Jerusalem in AD70, in fulfillment of Daniel 7.

The time has come for all futurists to stop "kicking against the goads" of the biblical doctrine of the first century Parousia of Christ; and begin to honor the three-fold inspired testimony of Jesus, his apostles, and the Old Testament prophets. The King has come and all the holy ones with him.7

---

7.   Zechariah 14:5, Jude 14

MATTHEW 16:27-28 = ISAIAH 59:17-21

The second text which we will identify as an Old Testament source for Jesus' prophecy in Matthew 16:27-28 is Isaiah 59:17-21. Below are the two passages, one after another.

Matthew 16:27
"For the Son of Man is going to come in the glory of His Father with His angels, and *will then repay every man according to his deeds".*

Isaiah 59:18,20
"According to their deeds, so He will repay... A Redeemer will come to Zion..."

Undeniably, Matthew's Son of Man is Isaiah's Redeemer who was prophesied to "come" (return) in both salvation and vengeance, to repay Israel *"according to their deeds".* The following chart powerfully illustrates the numerous parallels in these two prophesies.

MATTHEW 16:27-28	ISAIAH 59:17-21
Coming of the Son of Man (16:27)	Coming of the Redeemer (59:19-20)
Judgment of Christ (16:27)	Judgment of the Lord (59:18)
Coming in glory (16:27)	Coming in glory (59:19)
Judgment of every man (16:27)	Judgment of the wicked and the righteous (59:18-20)
Judgment according to their deeds (16:27)	Judgment according to their deeds (59:18)
To establish the kingdom (16:28)	To establish the New Covenant-kingdom (59:20-21)
Fulfilled in the lifetime of Jesus' first century disciples (16:28)	

This is truly convincing evidence that Isaiah 59:17-20 is in fact a prophetic source for Jesus' prophecy in Matthew 16:27-28. The significant thing about this, is that unlike Daniel 7, all futurist eschatology's agree that Isaiah 59:17-21 prophesies the second coming of Christ. Let me repeat that. *All futurist eschatology's agree that Isaiah 59:17-21 prophesies the second coming of Christ.* This majority agreement should not surprise us in the least, after all, it was inspired apostolic doctrine that established this interpretation. Specifically, it was the apostle Paul in his letter to the Romans who interpreted the second coming of Christ to be the fulfillment of the "coming of the Redeemer to Zion" in Isaiah 59. Notice the two passages followed by a comparative chart, illustrating the perfect parallels.

Romans 11:26-27

And so, all Israel will be saved; just as it is written, *"The Deliverer will come from Zion, he will remove ungodliness from Jacob." This is my covenant with them,* when I take away their sins. 1

Isaiah 59:20-21

A Redeemer will come to Zion, and to those who turn from transgression in Jacob, declares the Lord. As for Me, *this is My covenant with them,"* says the Lord....

ISAIAH 59:17-21	ROMANS 11:25-27
The judgment of Israel (to repay according to their works) (59:18)	The judgment of Israel (to remove ungodliness from Jacob) (11:26)
Salvation of Israel (59:17,20)	Salvation of Israel (11:26)
The coming of the Lord (59:20)	The coming of the Lord (11:26)
To bring righteousness (59:14-17)	To take away their sins (11:27)
To establish the New Covenant (59:21)	To establish the New Covenant (11:27)

Clearly, Paul's "Deliverer" is Isaiah's "Redeemer" who would return to Zion to establish the promised New Covenant with "all Israel", that is, with "those

---

1. I am indebted to Don K. Preston for these connections. The taking away of Israel's sins in Romans 11:27 (in fulfillment of Isaiah 59) is a direct allusion to Daniel 9:24, "to make an end of sin" (Daniel's "70 weeks prophecy"). But in Isaiah 59, Israel's sins would be taken away at the judgment of the nation for shedding innocent blood (59:3,7,12-18). Therefore, Daniel's 70-weeks- prophecy would be fulfilled when Israel was judged for shedding innocent blood. (See Matthew 23:29-38 for precisely when this would take place). Also, the taking away of Israel's sin in Romans 11:27 is a direct quotation of the "forgiving" and "pardoning" of Israel's sin promised in Isaiah 27:9. Israel's sin would be forgiven when her alter stones were pulverized like chalk stones (27:9), when the fortified city isolated and forsaken (27:10), and when their Maker would "not have compassion on them" (27:11). Isaiah 27 just like Isaiah 59 prophesied the salvation of Israel (through the forgiveness of sin) at the time of their judgment and destruction. In Matthew 24:31, Jesus quotes Isaiah 27:13 verbatim. At the sounding of the "great trumpet" Israel would be both saved (gathered) and punished (24:29) in his generation (24:34). This agrees perfectly with Matthew 16:27-28. Israel would be both judged and saved (rewarded) in the lifetime of Jesus' contemporary disciples. Thus, the second coming of Christ in Romans 11:25-27 fulfills the coming of the Son of Man in Matthew 16:27-28, the salvation and judgment of Israel in Isaiah 27, and establishment of the New Covenant through the day of vengeance in Isaiah 59.

who turn from transgression in Jacob."2 The fact is, the futurist admission that the second coming of Christ in Romans 11 is the fulfillment of the coming of the Lord to Zion in Isaiah 59, is devastating to their doctrine of a future bodily return of Jesus. And as we have noted above, this admission has been imposed upon them by the inspired interpretation of the apostle Paul, and therefore cannot be denied.

Therefore, since Romans 11:25-27 prophesied the second coming of Christ in fulfillment of Isaiah 59:17-21, but the coming of the Lord in Isaiah 59:17-21 is the coming of the Son of Man in Matthew 16:27-28, then the coming of the Son of Man in Matthew 16:27-28 must refer to the second coming of Christ in fulfillment of Isaiah 59. The following chart powerfully illustrates the parallels in all three passages.

MATTHEW 16:27-28	ISAIAH 59:17-21	Romans 11:25-27
The coming of the Son of Man (16:27)	The coming of the Lord (59:20)	The coming of the Lord (11:26)
As Judge (16:27)	As Redeemer (59:20)	As Deliverer (11:26)
Repay according to their deeds (16:27)	Repay according to their deeds (59:18)	Take away the sins of Jacob (11:26-27)
To establish the kingdom (16:28)	To establish the New Covenant (59:21)	To establish the New Covenant (11:26-27)
Life received (16:25)	Redemption received (59:20)	Salvation received (11:26)
Fulfilled in the lifetime of Jesus' first century disciples (16:28)		

Based on this evidence, consider the argument on the following page:

2. Ironically, the favorite futurist "proof text" for their belief in a future restoration/salvation of the entire nation of ethnic Israel (all Israel), clearly limits "all Israel" to "those who turn from transgression in Jacob". The context is clear, those who would not turn from transgression would become the adversary of the Lord who would be "repaid according to their deeds" at his coming. In other words, only those of all Israel who turned from their sins to their Redeemer would be saved, those who would not would not be saved. Also, see Romans 9:6-9 (the larger context for Romans 11) for the identity and the *limitation* of Pauls' "all Israel" in Romans 11.

-Matthew 16:27-28 = Isaiah 59:17-21

-But according to Paul in Romans 11:25-27, Isaiah 59:17-21 was a prophecy of the second coming of Christ for the salvation of all Israel.

-Therefore, Matthew 16:27-28 prophesied the second coming of Christ for the salvation of all Israel in fulfillment of Isaiah 59:17-21.

This being true, notice what *must* also be true....
-Matthew 16:27-28 prophesied the second coming of Christ for the salvation of all Israel in fulfillment of Isaiah 59:17-21.

-But according to Jesus, his second coming was to occur in the lifetime of his contemporary disciples. (Matthew 16:27-28)

-Therefore, the second coming of Christ for the salvation of all Israel in fulfillment of Isaiah 59:17-21 and Romans 11:25-27, must have taken place in the lifetime of Jesus' contemporary disciples.

This evidence and these arguments are irrefutable, and prove that the coming of the Son of Man in Matthew 16:27-28 must refer to the eschatological return of Yahweh to Zion - the New Jerusalem - to consummate and establish his New Covenant in fulfillment of Isaiah 59:17-21. And once again, *what absolutely must not be overlooked* is that the framework of "persecution-judgment-vindication" that we saw in Daniel 7 and Matthew 16 is present in Isaiah 59 also. 3 Israel's hands had become stained and defiled from shedding the blood of the righteous (59:3-7). As a result, the Lord would intercede for his saints (59:16) by bringing vengeance on his adversaries (59:18) and redemption to those who had "turned from transgression" through the establishment of the New Covenant (59:20-21). This three-fold thematic connection between Isaiah 59, Matthew 16, and Romans 11 cannot be easily broken. And as we shall see, the deeper we dig the tighter these cords become.

---

3.   To reiterate, one of the greatest interpretive oversights of the futurist camps concerning the doctrine of the second coming of Christ, is their failure to take into consideration the prophetic contexts surrounding many "second coming passages".

A CLOSER LOOK AT ISAIAH 59
VENGEANCE FOR SHEDDING INNOCENT BLOOD

As we have shown from   Daniel, by identifying *when* the themes/events surrounding the coming of the Son of Man were fulfilled, we can identify *when* the "coming" itself was fulfilled also. The same hermeneutic holds true for Isaiah. As we shall show, the eschatological themes/events found within the context of Isaiah 59 demand the fulfillment of the "coming of the Redeemer to Zion" (the second coming of Christ) in the lifetime of Jesus' first disciples. In the context of Isaiah 59, the coming of the Lord to Zion takes place at the time of:

1. The judgment of Israel for shedding innocent blood.
2. Israel's redemption/salvation.
3. The establishment of the New Covenant.

We will demonstrate from scripture that all three of these themes/events 1 find their fulfillment in the first century. But more specifically, they are all temporally connected to the fall of Jerusalem in AD70. This fact powerfully validates the *"time limitation"* that Jesus' placed upon his coming in Matthew 16:27-28 in fulfillment of Isaiah 59:17-21. We now begin to explore each of these themes/events.

One of the most significant and prevalent themes throughout all of scripture is "the vindication of the martyrs". 2 We could also call it, "vengeance for shedding innocent blood". In Isaiah 59, the prophet clearly identified the coming of the Lord to Zion as his coming in vengeance to judge Israel for shedding innocent blood. In other words, the Lord would come to vindicate his saints who had suffered at the hands of their own countrymen.

---

1. These three themes/events are eschatological to the core. In other words, they concern the time of the "end", or "last things". Significantly, each one of them is temporally connected to the "hope of Israel", that is, Israel's resurrection hope.
2. For an in depth and exhaustive study on this theme see, *"Revelation Realized Martyr Vindication from Genesis to Revelation"* by Samuel G. Dawson, *"The Avenging of the Apostles and Prophets"* by Arthur M. Ogden, and *"Who is This Babylon?"* by Don K. Preston. All three of these books also demonstrate that Babylon of Revelation was first century Old Covenant Jerusalem, and provide powerful evidence for the early date of John's Apocalypse.

Notice the larger context of the chapter....

> Isaiah 59:3,7,17-18,20
> For *your hands are defiled with blood* and your fingers with iniquity; your lips have spoken falsehood, your tongue mutters wickedness.... Their feet run to evil, and *they hasten to shed innocent blood;* their thoughts are thoughts of iniquity, devastation and destruction are in their highways.... He put on righteousness like a breastplate, and a helmet of salvation on His head; and *He put on garments of vengeance for clothing* and wrapped Himself with zeal as a mantle. *According to their deeds, so He will repay, wrath to His adversaries, recompense to His enemies;* to the coastlands He will make recompense....*A Redeemer will come to Zion, and to those who turn from transgression in Jacob,"* declares the Lord.

So, if we can determine *when* the judgment of Israel for shedding innocent blood takes place, we will have determined *when* the Redeemer comes to Zion. And to reiterate, since Paul interpreted Isaiah 59 as the second coming of Christ, then to identify *the time* of the vindication of the martyrs, is to identify *the time* that the second coming takes place. And it just so happens, that the Avenger of blood himself 3 leaves no room for private interpretation on the matter. Jesus undeniably placed the guilt of all the righteous blood that had been shed upon the earth since the foundation of the world, at the feet of *the Jews of his generation.*

> Matthew 23:29-31,34-36
> Woe to you, scribes and Pharisees, hypocrites! For you build the tombs of the prophets and adorn the monuments of the righteous, and say, 'If we had been living in the days of our fathers, we would not have been partners with them *in shedding the blood of the prophets.'* Therefore, behold, I am sending you prophets and wise men and scribes; some of them you will kill and crucify, and some of them you will scourge in your synagogues, and persecute from city to city, *so that upon you may fall the guilt of all the righteous blood shed on earth,* from the blood of righteous Abel to the blood of Zechariah, the son of Berechiah, whom you murdered between the temple and the altar. Truly I say to you, *all these things will come upon this generation.*

> Luke 11:47-50
> Woe to you! For *you build the tombs of the prophets, and it was your fathers who killed them.* So you are witnesses and approve the deeds of your fathers; because it was they who killed them, and you build their tombs. For this reason also the wisdom of God said, 'I will send to them

---

3.   1 Thessalonians 4:6

prophets and apostles, and some of them they will kill and some they will persecute, *so that the blood of all the prophets, shed since the foundation of the world, may be charged against this generation.*

Those who had scoffed at the vengeance of God would be judged according to their deeds in their own lifetime.

Matthew 27:24-25
When Pilate saw that he was accomplishing nothing, but rather that a riot was starting, he took water and washed his hands in front of the crowd, saying, *"I am innocent of this Man's blood; see to that yourselves." And all the people said, "His blood shall be on us and on our children!"*

Forty years later at the fall of Jerusalem in AD70, their request was granted. So, unless the "innocent blood" in Isaiah 59 can somehow be excluded from all the righteous blood shed on earth in Matthew 23, 4 then the coming of the Lord to Zion in Isaiah 59 to execute wrath on his adversaries and avenge the blood of his saints, must have been fulfilled at the coming of the Son of man in AD70. With this fact firmly established, consider the following argument:

-Israel would be judged for shedding innocent blood at the coming of the Lord to Zion, to take vengeance on his adversaries (Isaiah 59:17-20).
-But Israel was judged for shedding innocent blood - the blood of *all* the righteous - at the judgment of Jerusalem (AD70), in Jesus' generation. (Matthew 23:29-36)
-*Therefore, Israel was judged for shedding innocent blood in fulfillment of Isaiah 59 at the coming of the Lord to Zion to bring vengeance on his adversaries, at the judgment of Jerusalem (AD70) in Jesus' generation.*

But remember, according to the apostle Paul in Romans 11:25-27, the coming of the Lord to Zion would be fulfilled at the second coming of Christ. This leads us to our next argument:

---

4. It is not only illogical to say that the innocent blood of Isaiah 59 would not be included in "all the righteous blood shed on earth", but it's *thematically impossible* also. In both Isaiah 59 and Matthew 23 we find the biblical theme of "filling the measure of sin". In Isaiah 59:12, Israel acknowledges that their transgressions were, "multiplying before God". In Matthew 23:32, Jesus says, "Fill up, then, the measure of the guilt of your fathers." Thus, Israel's sin and guilt that had been multiplying for centuries would be judged in Jesus' generation. (Also see 1 Thessalonians 2:14-16).

-Israel would be judged for shedding innocent blood in fulfillment of Isaiah 59, at the coming of the Lord to Zion to bring vengeance on his adversaries (Israel) at the judgment of Jerusalem (AD70) in Jesus' generation.

-But, the coming of the Lord to Zion to bring vengeance on his adversaries (Israel) and judgment for shedding innocent blood in fulfillment of Isaiah 59, would be accomplished at the second coming of Christ (Romans 11:25-27).

-Therefore, the second coming of Christ was fulfilled at the judgment of Jerusalem in AD70, when the Lord came in vengeance on his adversaries to avenge the blood of his saints, in fulfillment of Isaiah 59.

Not surprisingly, this is exactly what Jesus predicted in his discourse on Mt. Olivet. Luke's account of that prophecy contains powerful evidence that Isaiah 59 lay behind the words of the Master. Below is the larger context of Isaiah 59 followed by Jesus' reiteration of that prophecy. Notice the perfect parallels....

> Isaiah 59:3,7,17-18,20
> For *your hands are defiled with blood* and your fingers with iniquity; your lips have spoken falsehood, your tongue mutters wickedness.... Their feet run to evil, and *they hasten to shed innocent blood*; their thoughts are thoughts of iniquity, devastation and destruction are in their highways.... He put on righteousness like a breastplate, and a helmet of salvation on His head; and *He put on garments of vengeance for clothing* and wrapped Himself with zeal as a mantle. *According to their deeds, so He will repay, wrath to His adversaries, recompense to His enemies;* to the coastlands He will make recompense.... *A Redeemer will come to Zion, and to those who turn from transgression in Jacob,"* declares the Lord.

> Luke 21:12,16,20,22-23,27,32
> But before all these things, *they will lay their hands on you and will persecute you, delivering you to the synagogues and prisons,* bringing you before kings and governors for My name's sake.... But you will be betrayed even by parents and brothers and relatives and friends, *and they will put some of you to death.... But when you see Jerusalem surrounded by armies, then recognize that her desolation is near.... because these are days of vengeance, so that all things which are written will be fulfilled.* Woe to those who are pregnant and to those who are nursing babies in those days; *for there will be great distress upon the land and wrath to this people....* Then they will see *the Son of Man coming in a cloud with power and great glory....* Truly I say to you, *this generation will not pass away until all things take place.*

The following chart clearly illustrates the fulfillment of Isaiah 59 in AD70. 5

ISAIAH 59	LUKE 21
The coming of the Lord to Zion (59:20)	The coming of the Son of Man to Jerusalem (21:27)
Judgment for shedding innocent blood (59:7,18)	Judgment for shedding innocent blood (21:12-20)
Salvation for the righteous (59:16,20-21)	Redemption for the righteous (21:28)
Vengeance and wrath upon his adversaries (Israel) (59:17-18)	The days of vengeance and wrath upon Jerusalem and her people (21:22-24)
	Fulfilled at the fall of Jerusalem in Jesus' generation (AD70) (21:32)

The fact that the innocent blood of the martyrs was avenged at the judgment of Old Covenant Israel in AD70, *limits* the second coming of Christ, which would accomplish that judgment, in both Isaiah 59 and Matthew 16:27-28, *to the same time and same event.* Thus, Christ appeared a second time *with salvation* at the fall of Jerusalem in AD70. He was "coming quickly", and his "reward was with him."6

---

5. The parallels between Jesus' Olivet discourse and Isaiah 59 could be multiplied if Matthew 23 (which sets the context for the discourse) is taken into consideration also.
6. Revelation 22:12

THE DAY OF SALVATION

Although it is true that the coming of the Lord in Isaiah 59 is temporally connected to Israel's "days of vengeance" (martyr vindication), it is equally true that the coming of the Lord in Isaiah 59 is temporally connected to Israel's "day of salvation" (day of redemption). In anticipation of the second coming of Christ in fulfillment of Isaiah 59 Paul says, *"And so, all Israel will be saved; just as it is written, "The Deliverer will come from Zion.* 1 Biblically speaking, Israel's day of salvation would come at the second coming of Christ, concurrent with her time of great distress.2

Commenting on this prophetic paradox, N.T. Wright says, "There was, in other words, a belief hammered out.... that Israel's sufferings might be, not merely a state *from* which she would, in YHWY's good time, be saved and redeemed, but paradoxically, under certain circumstances and in certain sense, part of the means *by* which that redemption would be affected."3 In a more simplified statement, McKnight says, "Thematically, Jesus' vision of AD70 concerned both redemption and judgment."4 The point is, the time of Israel's salvation cannot be separated from the second coming of Christ in the judgment of Old Covenant Israel. Although we have thoroughly established a first century second coming of Christ through the theme of martyr vindication, it is important that we prove our position from yet another angle. Thus, to determine *the time* of Israel's salvation (redemption), is to determine *the time* that the Redeemer came (returned) to Zion, a second time.

Despite popular opinion, Jesus did not complete his work of salvation at either his death or his resurrection. If he did, then his coming again, which would bring salvation, was accomplished at that time also. Clearly that scenario is nonsensical.5

---

1. Romans 11:26, in fulfillment of Isaiah 59:20.
2. Luke 21:20-23, in fulfillment of Jeremiah 30:7.
3. N.T. Wright, *Jesus and the Victory of God,* (Minneapolis; Fortress, 1996), p.591
4. Scott McKnight, *A New Vision For Israel,* (Grand Rapids; Eerdmans, 1999), p.12
5. This demonstrates the utter confusion within most futurist eschatology's. On one hand, they insist that salvation was fully accomplished (perfected) at the cross. On the other, they fully reject that the second coming of Christ - to bring salvation - has taken place. They therefore separate salvation from the coming of the Savior who brings salvation. Biblically, salvation was to be fully applied at the second coming of Christ. Wherever we place the second coming, is *when* salvation is made available; it's that simple.

The message that shines forth from the pages of the New Testament, even decades after the cross, is that the first fruit generation of Christians were still anticipating the "outcome 6 of their faith, the salvation of their souls"; 7 which according to Peter, was "ready 8 to be revealed" in those last times. 9 Read carefully the words of the fisher-of-men from Galilee....

> 1 Peter 1:3-5,9
> Blessed be the God and Father of our Lord Jesus Christ, who according to His great mercy *has caused us to be born again to a living hope* through the resurrection of Jesus Christ from the dead, to obtain an inheritance which is imperishable and undefiled and will not fade away, reserved in heaven for you, who are protected by the power of God through faith *for a salvation ready to be revealed in the last time....* obtaining as the outcome of your faith *the salvation of your souls.*

Peter goes on to identify the salvation of their souls as the "glories" and the "grace" that would be brought to his generation at the revelation 10 of Jesus Christ. For Peter, the *salvation of Israel* at the coming of the Lord, was a first century expectation.

> 1 Peter 1:10-11,13
> *As to this salvation, the prophets who prophesied of the grace that would come to you* made careful searches and inquiries, seeking to know what person or time the Spirit of Christ within them was indicating as He predicted the sufferings of Christ and *the glories to follow....* Therefore.... fix your

---

6. The word translated as "outcome" is the Greek word, "telos" and means, "the end, point of termination, the aim or purpose, the goal". For Peter, the goal and purpose of their faith was to receive the salvation of their souls. This purpose had clearly not been fully accomplished at the time that Peter wrote his first epistle.
7. 1 Peter 1:9
8. The Greek word translated as "ready" in 1 Peter 1:5 is "hetoimos", which means "prepared, to be in readiness" (Thayer's). It carries the idea of being both mentally and temporally prepared/ready.
9. "The last time" of 1 Peter 1:5 is identified as "these (Peter's) last times" in 1 Peter 1:20. Thus, the end goal of their salvation was ready to be revealed in Peter's days.
10. The perfect parallel between Hebrews 9 and 1 Peter 1 should not be missed. Both writers clearly teach that *salvation* was to be received and therefore consummated at the appearing/revelation of Christ. Both Peter and the Hebrews writer (10:36-39) taught and expected the coming of Christ *with salvation* in their lifetime.

hope completely on *the grace to be brought to you at the revelation of Jesus Christ.*

The writer of Hebrews agreed, the second appearing of Christ was to bring, and therefore consummate, Israel's promised salvation 11 ....

> Hebrews 9:28
> So Christ also, having been offered once to bear the sins of many, *will appear a second time for salvation without reference to sin, to those who eagerly await Him.*

And just like Peter, the Hebrews writer fully expected that their promised soul-salvation was about to be received in a "very little while", at the second coming of Jesus Christ.

> Hebrews 10:36-37
> For you have need of endurance, so that when you have done the will of God, you may receive *what was promised.* For yet *in a very little while, He who is coming will come, and will not delay....* But we are not of those who shrink back to destruction, but of those who have faith *to the preserving of the soul.*

In his letter to the Romans, the apostle to the Gentiles saw it the exact same way. Salvation had at that time not yet fully arrived but was drawing ever nearer....

> Romans 13:11-12
> Do this, knowing the time, that it is already the hour for you to awaken from sleep; for *now salvation is nearer to us than when we believed.* The night is almost gone and *the day is near.*

Concerning "the day" that was near, in chapter 49:8-10 of Isaiah, the prophet foretold *a day* when Israel's salvation would arrive. In that day, the land would be restored, they would no longer hunger or thirst, the scorching heat would no

---

11. The "second appearing" of Christ in Hebrews 9:28 fits into the larger context of the chapter concerning the Day of Atonement. In verses 24-26 we see Jesus as high priest offering up himself as the sacrifice and bringing his own blood into the most holy place. Thus, the "appearing a second time" (literally, "out of second") is the return of the high priest from the most holy place to consummate the atonement and complete salvation for Israel, once for all time.

longer strike them down, and the Lord their God would guide them to springs of living water. 12 In 2 Corinthians 6:2 Paul quotes Isaiah 49:8 verbatim and applies the prophecy to his day. Paul said, "At the acceptable time I listened to you, and *on the day of salvation* I helped you." Behold, *now is the acceptable time, behold, now is the day of salvation.*"13 According to Paul, Israel's day of salvation had begun through the gospel, and what was "near" and "ready to be revealed" in those "last times", was its full arrival.

Paul went so far as saying that by receiving the Holy Spirit they had received a pledge,14 guaranteeing them the full measure of their salvation-inheritance. In his letter to the Ephesians, Paul used the terms salvation and redemption synonymously. The gospel was the good news of their coming salvation, and through the Spirit they were sealed for their coming redemption. The *day of salvation* would be their *day of redemption.*

> Ephesians 1:13-14, 4:30
> In Him, you also, after listening to the message of truth, *the gospel of your salvation* - having also believed, *you were sealed in Him with the Holy Spirit of promise, who is given as a pledge of our inheritance,* with a view to the redemption of God's own possession, to the praise of His glory.... Do not grieve the Holy Spirit of God, *by whom you were sealed for the day of redemption.*

The consistent testimony of the New Testament writers was that the salvation of their souls (their redemption) was about to be fully received at the second coming of Christ, in the day of salvation. It should not surprise us then, that Jesus connects the "day of redemption" (salvation) with his coming in clouds to establish the kingdom, and places its fulfillment at the destruction of Jerusalem in AD70.

---

12. Compare Isaiah 49:10 with Revelation 7:16-17 and 21:4-6.
13. 2 Corinthians 6:2 is a direct quotation of Isaiah 49:8. This means that Israel's Messianic "day of salvation" had arrived in Pauls' lifetime.
14. The Greek word translated "pledge" is "arrabon", and means "an earnest, money which in purchases is given as a pledge or down payment that the full amount will subsequently be paid". Vines Expository Dictionary defines arrabon as, "earnest-money" deposited by the purchaser and forfeited if the purchase was not completed.... In modern Greek "arrabona" is an "engagement ring." We should therefore understand the gift of the Holy Spirit as the dowry which guaranteed Yahweh's remarriage to Israel; in that first century generation. This make perfect sense in light of the message of both John the Baptist and Jesus concerning the remarriage of Israel.

Luke 21:20,27-28,31-32

But *when you see Jerusalem surrounded by armies, then recognize that her desolation is near*.... Then they will see the Son of Man coming in a cloud with power and great glory. But *when these things begin to take place, straighten up and lift up your heads, because your redemption is drawing near*.... So you also, *when you see these things happening, recognize that the kingdom of God is near.* Truly I say to you, *this generation will not pass away until all things take place.*

Jesus' words in Luke 21 are his promise and guarantee to fulfill the prophecy of Isaiah 59 - the coming of the Redeemer to Zion to bring salvation to Israel - within the lifetime of his first disciples. With this established, consider the following argument:

-The salvation of Israel in fulfillment of Isaiah 59 was to be accomplished at the second coming of the Lord to Zion.

-But, the salvation of Israel in Isaiah 59 was accomplished in Jesus' generation, at the destruction of Jerusalem in AD70. (Hebrews 9:28, 10:37-39, Luke 21:20-32)

-*Therefore, the salvation of Israel at the second coming of the Lord to Zion in fulfillment of Isaiah 59, was accomplished in Jesus' generation, at the fall of Jerusalem in AD70.*

This conclusion agrees perfectly with Jesus' words in Matthew 16:27-28. In fulfillment of Isaiah 59, Jesus promised to *come* (return) *with reward* (salvation) in the lifetime of his contemporary disciples. His coming in his kingdom was his coming to bring salvation.... his reward was with him.

THE ARRIVAL OF THE NEW COVENANT

The third theme/event that is both thematically and temporally connected to the coming of the Lord in Isaiah 59, is the full arrival and establishment of Israel's promised *New Covenant*. In agreement with and in expectation of Isaiah 59, Paul taught that the full arrival of Israel's New Covenant - to take away their sin - would be accomplished at the second coming of Christ. Notice again the perfect parallels.

> Isaiah 59:20-21
> *A Redeemer will come to Zion,* and to those who turn from transgression in Jacob," declares the Lord. As for Me, *this is My covenant with them....*"

> Romans 11:26-27
> And so all Israel will be saved; just as it is written, *"The Deliverer will come from Zion,* He will remove ungodliness from Jacob." *This is my covenant with them,* when I take away their sins.

Despite the clear testimony of scripture, much of Christianity is woefully confused concerning *the time* for the full arrival of the New Covenant. Although it is true that through the death of Christ the New Covenant was inaugurated, it is equally true that the Covenant had not reached perfection at that time.1 In fact, the High-Priesthood of Jesus was the "guarantee"2 of its then-future consummation. Not until the defeat of his enemies at his coming (return) from Zion would Christ fully establish the New Covenant, resulting in the removal of sin.3 So then, by identifying *the time* that the New Covenant fully arrived, we will by implication identify *the time* that the second coming of Christ, as Redeemer of Israel, was fulfilled.

---

1. Luke 22:20, Hebrews 10:19-20. Much of Christianity today believes that the New Covenant fully arrived at either the cross of Christ or the day of Pentecost. Yet scripture is abundantly clear that the New Covenant would not fully arrive until the second coming of Christ. The church world as a whole seems blissfully ignorant of the fact that by postponing the second coming of Christ, they are postponing the establishment of the New Covenant and the   full removal of sin! The second coming of Christ was to bring to perfection the New Covenant dispensation on earth in fulfillment of the Lord's model-prayer, "your will be done, on earth as it is in heaven".
2. Hebrews 7:20-22
3. Hebrews 10:11-17, Romans 11:25-27

To begin with, the writer of Hebrews tells us that in his days, that is, in *those* last days, 4 the covenants were changing, that is, they were transitioning. Notice specifically the present tenses in the following verses.

> Hebrews 8:13
> "....He has made *the first* obsolete. But *whatever is becoming obsolete and growing old is ready to disappear*".

> Hebrews 10:9
> "....*He takes away the first in order to establish the second*".

Through the one-for-all-time sacrifice of the body of Christ the first Covenant had become obsolete (old) and was at that time being taken away, *in order that* (so that) the New (second) Covenant could be fully established. What this means is that only when the Old Covenant was fully removed through the fulfillment of all prophecy,5 would the New Covenant be fully established and its blessings fully received.

Now ask yourself this question: Do you know of any serious student of the bible who would insist that the Old Covenant has not yet been taken away, that is, has not yet been made covenantally insignificant? I sure hope not! So, since the Old Covenant has already been removed, then the New Covenant must already be fully established! But when did that take place? When did the New Covenant arrive in perfection? The apostle Paul is clear as crystal concerning *the time* when the Covenant-hope of Israel was to be fulfilled.

In his letter to the churches in Galatia, Paul said that Hagar and Sarah allegorically represented the *two Covenants*....

> Galatians 4:22-24
> For it is written that Abraham had two sons, one by *the bondwoman* and one by *the free woman*. But the son by the bondwoman was born according to *the flesh*, and the son by the free woman through *the promise*. This is allegorically speaking, for *these women are two covenants* ....

---

4. Hebrews 1:1-2. It was in the "last days" of the Old Covenant age that God spoke in (through) His Son.
5. Matthew 5:17-18 Luke 21:20-33

61

Paul went on to say that Mount Sinai (the mountain that can be touched) and first century Jerusalem represented the Old Covenant (Hagar), while the Jerusalem from above represented the New Covenant, (Sarah).

Galatians 4:25

Now *this Hagar is Mount Sinai in Arabia and corresponds to the present Jerusalem,* for she is in slavery with her children.

Galatians 4:26
But *the Jerusalem above is free; she is our mother.*

We see then that these two cities (old and new Jerusalem) correspond to two mountains, *which represent the two covenants.* With this understanding, consider what the writer of Hebrews says.

Hebrews 12:18-19,22
For you have not come to *a mountain that can be touched and to a blazing fire, and to darkness and gloom and whirlwind,* and to the blast of a trumpet and the sound of words which sound was such that those who heard begged that no further word be spoken to them.... But *you have come to Mount Zion and to the city of the living God, the heavenly Jerusalem...."*

We must allow the words of Paul in Galatians to be the inspired commentary on this Hebrews passage. By contrasting the two city-mountains the Hebrews writer is contrasting the two covenants. The mountain that "can be touched" was Mount Sinai, earthly Jerusalem, *the Old Covenant.* Mount Zion was the "Jerusalem above", heavenly Jerusalem, *the New Covenant.* This means that what was being shaken and removed in Hebrews 12 was the Old Covenant,6 including the entire Jewish world governed and empowered through the Law of that Covenant. But, through that shaking and removal, the New Covenant was being received *as* the kingdom of God. The time had come for the saints to *possess* the kingdom and the blessings of the New Covenant.

Hebrews 12:26-27
"And His voice shook the earth then, but now He has promised,
saying, "Yet once more, I will shake not only the earth, but also the

---

6. Hebrews 12:18-20 is a quotation of Exodus 19:12-13, while Hebrews 12:26 is a quotation of Haggai 2:6-7,21-22. The conflation of these Old Testament passages in the context of Hebrews 12 is significant. The power and authority of the old "Jewish world" - that old "heaven and earth" - was shaken and removed so that the power and authority (the forgiveness of sin and dominion over death) of the New Covenant world in Christ would be established.

heaven" This expression, "Yet once more," denotes *the removing of those things which can be shaken,* as of created things, *so that those things which cannot be shaken may remain. Therefore, since we receive a kingdom which cannot be shaken...."*

Therefore, the promised New Covenant would be established with Israel through the arrival of their promised kingdom. But as we have already seen, the kingdom would fully arrive, and thus be fully received, at the judgment of Israel in AD70. Recall the words of Jesus in his parable of the vineyard....

Matthew 21:40-41,43
Therefore, when the owner of the vineyard comes, what will he do to those vine-growers? They said to Him, *He will bring those wretches to a wretched end, and will rent out the vineyard to other vine-growers* who will pay him the proceeds at the proper seasons.... Therefore, I say to you, *the kingdom of God will be taken away from you and given to a people,* producing the fruit of it.... When the chief priests and the Pharisees heard His parables, *they understood that He was speaking about them.*

The interpretation of this parable was no mystery then, (21:45) nor should it be now. As punishment for their murder of the Son and his messengers, as well as their failure to bring forth fruit through repentance (21:33-39), the kingdom would be taken from the Jews and given to another people. In Jesus' very next parable, this *"kingdom transfer"* is reiterated through slightly different imagery. As punishment for their murder of the servants and their rejection of the call to their wedding, 7 the Jews would suffer a terrible destruction. Those upon whom the Stone would fall, would also be burned with fire.8

Matthew 22:2-3,7
The kingdom of heaven may be compared to *a king who gave a wedding feast for his son.* And he sent out his slaves to call those who had been

---

7.   Recall our comments above, that the Holy Spirit given as a "pledge" should be seen in the context of a marriage dowry. Thus, for Jesus to teach that the marriage of the Son to Israel was to be consummated in that generation (surrounding the destruction of Jerusalem in AD70), is perfectly consistent with what Paul taught; that the Spirit was their "pledge" (guarantee) that their salvation (inheritance) was to be consummated in their lifetime. If the Lord did not return to "make good" on the pledge, then the promise of salvation failed.
8.   Compare this judgment of the Jews by *"by fire"* in Matthew 22 with Matthew 3:7-12, Luke 3:7-18, and Revelation 17.

invited to the wedding feast, and *they were unwilling to come.* Again, he sent out other slaves saying, *'Tell those who have been invited, "Behold, I have prepared my dinner;* my oxen and my fattened livestock are all butchered and everything is ready; come to the wedding feast." *But they paid no attention* and went their way, one to his own farm, another to his business, and *the rest seized his slaves and mistreated them and killed them.* But the king was enraged, and *he sent his armies and destroyed those murderers and set their city on fire.*

By conflating these two parables we can see that the kingdom was taken from the Jews and given to other people *when the murderers (the persecutors of the righteous) were destroyed and their city burned with fire.* The following chart illustrates that the two parables communicate only one message, applicable for only one generation; the judgment of Jerusalem in AD70.

MATTHEW 21:33-45	MATTHEW 22:1-14
A Landowner, his slaves and his Son (21:33-37)	A King, his slaves and his Son (22:2-3)
The call to bear fruit rejected (21:34-35)	The call to the wedding rejected (22:3)
Slaves and Son killed by the vine-growers (21:35-39)	Slaves killed by those invited to the wedding (22:3-6)
Landowner destroys those wretches (21:41)	King destroys those murderers (22:7)
The kingdom of those wretches taken away (21:43)	The city of those wretches burned with fire (22:7)
"Other people" possess the kingdom (21:43)	The "good" dinner guests feast with the King (22:10)

Therefore, since the New Covenant would be established through the arrival of the kingdom (Hebrews 12), and since the kingdom would arrive through the destruction of Jerusalem (Matthew 22); then the New Covenant must have been established at the judgment and destruction of Jerusalem in AD70. In Luke's account of the Olivet discourse, Jesus reiterates the narrative of these parables, and once again limits their fulfillment to the lifetime of his contemporary generation.

Luke 21:20-22,31-32
But *when you see Jerusalem surrounded by armies, then recognize that her desolation is near.... because these are days of vengeance,* so that all things which are written will be fulfilled.... So you also, *when you see these things happening, recognize that the kingdom of God is near.* Truly I say to you, *this generation will not pass away until all things take place.*

Thus, Luke 21 agrees perfectly with the parables of Jesus as well as many of the New Testament letters. 9 In view of what we have established above, consider the following argument:

-Israel's New Covenant in Isaiah 59 would be fully established through the arrival of the kingdom of God. (Hebrews 12:18-28)

-But, the kingdom of God arrived through the destruction of Jerusalem in AD70. (Matthew 21:33-45, Matthew 22:1-14, Luke 21:20-32)

-Therefore, Israel's New Covenant in Isaiah 59 was fully established through the destruction of Jerusalem in AD70.

Now, let's apply this to the coming of the Lord in Isaiah 59....
-Israel's New Covenant was fully established through the destruction of Jerusalem in AD70.

-But Israel's New Covenant would be fully established at the second coming of Christ for the salvation of all (the remnant) Israel. (Isaiah 59:20-21, Romans 11:25-27)

-Therefore, the second coming of Christ was fulfilled at the destruction of Jerusalem in AD70, which brought salvation to the remnant of Israel through the consummation of their New Covenant in fulfillment of Isaiah 59 and Romans 11.

In conclusion: Matthew 16:27-28 prophesied the first century second coming of Christ to avenge the blood of his saints, and to consummate the salvation of Israel through the perfection of her New Covenant, in fulfillment of Isaiah 59. Once again, the biblical doctrine of the first century second coming of Christ has been confirmed and vindicated from the pages of holy scripture.

---

9. For example, in Hebrews 9:6-11 we see that the kingdom (the time of reformation) would come through the removal of the Old Covenant. Access into the "holy place" (the greater and more perfect tabernacle) would only be granted when the "first tabernacle" (the tabernacle made with hands) had lost its "standing" (its covenant significance). Thus, when the Old Covenant system was removed (fulfilled and destroyed) the time of reformation was complete, and the New Covenant-kingdom arrived. I highly recommend Don K. Preston's book, *"The End of The Law - Torah to Telos - The Passing of the Law of Moses"* for a scholarly investigation into the relationship between the temple, the Law, the kingdom, and the end of the age in AD70.

MATTHEW 16:27-28 = ISAIAH 40:10 & ISAIAH 62:11

The third and fourth Old Testament passages that serve as a source for Jesus' prophecy in Matthew 16:27-28 are Isaiah 40:10 and 62:11, which we will investigate together. All three texts are quoted below:

> Isaiah 40:5,10
> Then *the glory of the Lord will be revealed, and all flesh will see it together;* for the mouth of the Lord has spoken." Behold, *the Lord God will come with might, with His arm ruling for Him.* Behold, *His reward is with Him, and His recompense before Him.*

> Isaiah 62:2,11
> *The nations will see your righteousness, and all kings your glory;* and you will be called by a new name which the mouth of the Lord will designate.... Behold, the Lord has proclaimed to the end of the earth, say to the daughter of Zion, *Lo, your salvation comes; behold His reward is with Him, and His recompense before Him.*

> Matthew 16:27-28 (NKJV)
> For *the Son of Man will come in the glory of His Father* with His angels, and *then He will reward each according to his works*.... there are some standing here who shall not taste death till they see *the Son of Man coming in His kingdom.*

Isaiah's imagery and language of the coming of the Lord in *glory* with his *arm ruling for him*, is a beautiful parallel to the Son of Man coming in his *kingdom*, in *the glory* of his Father.[1] Also, Isaiah's mention of *reward* in the context of "*all flesh*", corresponds to the "*rewarding of every man*" in Matthew.

The following chart will help to illustrate that Jesus in Matthew 16:27-28 was quoting from Isaiah's prophecies, and promised their fulfillment within the lifetime of the disciples to whom he was speaking.

---

1. See Don K. Preston's book, *"Like Father Like Son, on Clouds of Glory"* for an exhaustive and powerful study on what Jesus meant by the "glory of the Father" in the context of his Parousia, as well as *when* and in *what manner* the "day of the Lord" was to be fulfilled in the first century generation.

66

MATTHEW 16:27-28	ISAIAH 40:10	ISAIAH 62:11
Coming of the Son of Man (16:27)	Coming of the Lord (40:10)	Coming of the Lord (62:11)
Coming with reward (16:27)	Coming with reward (40:10)	Coming with reward (62:11)
In glory (16:27)	In glory (40:5)	In glory (62:2)
To establish the kingdom (16:28)	To establish his kingdom in Zion (40:10)	To establish his kingdom in Zion (62:1-2,11-12)
Fulfilled in the lifetime of Jesus' first century disciples (16:28)		

Both Isaiah 40:10 and 62:11 are without a doubt part of the prophetic source behind Jesus' words in Matthew 16:27-28. Therefore, consider the following argument:

-Matthew 16:27-28 = Isaiah 40:10 and Isaiah 62:11

-But, Isaiah 40:10 and 62:11 prophesied the salvation of Israel at the second coming of the Lord, the covenant-return of Yahweh.

-Therefore, Matthew 16:27-28 prophesied the second coming of Christ in fulfillment of Isaiah 40:10 and 62:11, and promised its accomplishment within the lifetime of Jesus' contemporary disciples.

Although we are more than confident that the argument above supports itself in identifying Matthew 16:27-28 as the fulfillment of Isaiah 40:10 and 62:11, we will once again allow the larger context of these prophesies to furnish additional support to this conclusion. As we shall see, the fact that John was the voice of the messenger who came preaching in the wilderness, has significant implications for our understanding of the gospel of the kingdom, and the doctrine of the second coming of Christ.

ISAIAH, THE BAPTIST AND
THE GOSPEL OF THE KINGDOM

Isaiah's prophecy to "make ready (prepare) the way of the Lord" is probably known best through the testimony of John the Baptist; and significantly, in one way or another, all four gospel writers record that testimony.1 When asked by the priests and Levites from Jerusalem concerning himself; John, being aware of his unique mission and message, had these words to say to the leaders of Israel....

> John 1:23
> "....*I am a voice of one crying in the wilderness*, make straight the way of the Lord, as Isaiah the prophet said."2

> Matthew 3:3-4
> *The voice of one crying in the wilderness, make ready the way of the Lord,* make his paths straight. Now John himself..."

> Mark 1:3-4
> *The voice of one crying in the wilderness, make ready the way of the Lord,* make his paths straight. John the Baptist appeared..."

> Luke 3:2,4
> In the high priesthood of Annas and Caiaphas, the word of God came to John, the son of Zacharias, in the wilderness.... As it is written in the book of the words of Isaiah the prophet, *the voice of one crying in the wilderness, make ready the way of the Lord,* make his paths straight.

Although John was the "voice" that Isaiah predicted would be heard before the coming of the Lord, John's primary purpose was not to prepare *the way* for the incarnation-coming 3 of Jesus as the Son of Joseph. Contrary to popular opinion, John was preparing a spiritual highway for the final return of Yahweh

---

1. This fact alone should cause us to consider the importance of John's ministry in Israel's last day's narrative.
2. Isaiah 40:3. The fact that John came to prepare the way of the Lord and the hearts of the people *for the second coming of Christ* and not his incarnation (first) coming, cannot be overemphasized.
3. By "incarnation-coming", I mean his coming to earth in the form of a servant to die as the sacrifice for sin.

to establish his kingdom and to bring salvation to Israel, in fulfillment of Isaiah 40 and Isaiah 62. 4 Notice the larger context of Isaiah.

> Isaiah 40:3-5,10-11
> *A voice is calling, Clear the way for the Lord in the wilderness; make smooth in the desert a highway for our God.* Let every valley be lifted up, and every mountain and hill be made low; and let the rough ground become a plain, and the rugged terrain a broad valley; *then the glory of the Lord will be revealed, and all flesh will see it together;* for the mouth of the Lord has spoken.... Behold, *the Lord God will come with might, with His arm ruling for Him. Behold, His reward is with Him* and His recompense before Him. Like a shepherd He will tend His flock, *in His arm He will gather the lambs* and carry them in His bosom; He will gently lead the nursing ewes.

To say it plainly, John's message was that the *return* of the covenant-presence of Yahweh *through the second coming of Christ* was about be fulfilled; therefore repent. This has far reaching implications for what both John and Jesus meant by "the kingdom of heaven is at hand". If John was the harbinger of the second coming of Christ, which he was, then the good news (gospel) of the kingdom was that Christ was about to fully establish his Messianic reign among Israel, in fulfillment of the Messianic hope. With this understanding in mind, please read the following passages.

> Matthew 3:1-2
> Now in those days *John the Baptist came* preaching in the wilderness of Judea, *saying, "Repent, for the kingdom of heaven is at hand."*

> Matthew 4:17
> From that time, *Jesus began to preach and say, "Repent, for the kingdom of heaven is at hand.*

---

4. John was sent primarily to prepare Israel for the second coming of Christ in the sight of "all flesh" (40:5), in order that he might save the remnant and gather them into his kingdom at the time of the Messianic remarriage (40:9-11, 62:10-12). In Don K. Preston's book, *"Elijah Has Come, A Solution to Romans 11:25-27",* Preston masterfully develops the connections between eschatology, the ministry and message of John, and the fulfillment of all prophecy in the first century. I am indebted to Don for those connections from which I draw upon here.

Mark 1:14-15
Now after John had been taken into custody, *Jesus came into Galilee,
preaching the gospel of God, and saying, "The time is fulfilled, and the kingdom
of God is at hand;* repent and believe in the gospel."

Based on the points just made, consider the following argument:
-Isaiah prophesied a "voice" would come crying in the wilderness to prepare
the way for the *second coming* of Christ in his kingdom.

-But John was that "voice", and John's message was, "the kingdom of heaven   is
at hand".

*-Therefore, the second coming of Christ in his kingdom in fulfillment of Isaiah 40 and Isaiah
62 was truly "at hand" in the first century.*

This agrees perfectly with the words of Jesus in Matthew 16:27-28. As we have
seen, Jesus promised that his coming in his kingdom in fulfillment of Old
Testament prophecy, was about be accomplished in the lifetime of his
contemporary disciples. We have seen that both Isaiah 40:10 and Isaiah 62:11
served as primary prophetic sources for the coming of the Son of Man in Matthew
16:27-28. John's identity as the "voice" provides powerful biblical evidence that
the covenant-return of Yahweh in fulfillment of Isaiah's prophecies, was about to
take place through the second coming of Christ in the first century.

But that's not all concerning the message of the Baptist. John was not only the
voice of Isaiah, he was the messenger of Malachi. This too has far reaching
implications.

JOHN, MALACHI AND THE TIME OF HARVEST

Prior to the birth of John, an angel of the Lord appeared to his father Zacharias to inform him of things to come concerning his son. His name would be John, and he would be a prophet of the Most High God. He would go before the Lord as forerunner, in the spirit and power of Elijah. What a wonderful message this must have been for old Zacharias.

> Luke 1:17
> It is he who will go *as a forerunner before Him in the spirit and power of Elijah,*
> to turn the hearts of the fathers back to the children and the disobedient
> to the attitude of the righteous, *so as to make ready a people*
> *prepared for the Lord.*

Approximately nine months later when John was brought to be circumcised according to the Law, Zacharias was filled with the Spirit and prophesied....

> Luke 1:76
> And you, child, will be called the prophet of the Most High; for *you*
> *will go on before the Lord to prepare His ways.*1

It is significant that both the angel and Zacharias quote from the book of Malachi 2 concerning the mission and message of John. The reason this is significant is because just like in Isaiah, the coming of the Lord in Malachi did not refer to the incarnation-coming of Jesus into the lower-world of flesh. Instead, Malachi prophesied the coming of the Lord in judgment to destroy that world of flesh by fire.

> Malachi 4:1,5
> For behold, *the day is coming, burning like a furnace;* and all the arrogant

---

1. In Luke 1:68, when Zachariah says the Lord has "*visited* and redeemed his people...", he is directly alluding to Genesis 50:24 where Joseph prophesied that the Lord would *visit* his brethren and bring them out of Egypt. In Exodus 4:31, in fulfillment of this prophecy of Joseph, we see that the Lord had *visited* the children of Israel by sending Moses to deliver them from Egypt through the exodus. Thus, through the ministry of John the Baptist, Yahweh was *visiting* his people in preparation for a *second exodus*. The theme of the second exodus is prominent throughout Luke's gospel.
2. Malachi 4:4-6 (Luke 1:17), Malachi 3:1 (Luke 1:76)

and every evildoer will be chaff... Behold, *I am going to send you Elijah the prophet before the coming of the great and terrible day of the Lord.* 3

In other words, like Isaiah, Malachi prophesied the second coming of Christ. But on top of that, Malachi predicted the coming of *a messenger* who would prepare the way for the Lord's coming. However, unlike the *voice* in Isaiah who trumpets the good news of Israel's salvation, the *messenger* in Malachi sounds the trumpet of alarm 4 to warn Israel of the judgment to come at the great and terrible day of the Lord. And undeniably, John was that messenger....

> Mark 1:2,4
> "As it is written in Isaiah the prophet: Behold, *I send my messenger ahead of you, who will prepare your way.... John the Baptist appeared* in the wilderness...."

> Luke 7:24,27
> "When the messengers of John had left, *he began to speak to the crowds about John....* This is the one about whom it is written, 'Behold, *I send my messenger ahead of you, who will prepare your way before you.*

Therefore, John as *both* the voice and the messenger carried a good news/bad news message for Israel, to be fulfilled at the second coming of Christ. The good news was that the kingdom of heaven was at hand. The bad news was, so was the great and terrible day of the Lord. But there's more. If John was Malachi's messenger, which he was, then John was Elijah. At least that's the way Jesus saw it.

---

3. Malachi 3:2-3, 4:1. This coming of the Lord *in fire* at the day of the Lord is reiterated in 2 Peter 3, when "heaven and earth" (the "kosmos" of Judaism) is burned with fire at the second coming of Christ. The idea that the Old Covenant world of Judaism represents the "world of flesh" is evident by Peter's allusion to Genesis 6:13 (the end of all flesh) in 1 Peter 4:7, "the end of all things is at hand". For Peter, the destruction of Judaism and its followers by fire was the destruction of the "world (kosmos) of flesh". Malachi, John, and Peter all preached the same message.
4. John came to Israel as a "last day's watchman". John saw the *sword of the Lord* coming upon Israel and he sounded the trumpet of the gospel of the kingdom to warn the people. Paul did the same thing. Compare Ezekiel 33:1-5 with Acts 17:1-18:6 and the message of John, specifically to the religious leaders of Paul's day.

Matthew 11:10,14

This is the one about whom it is written, 'Behold, *I send my messenger ahead of you,* who will prepare your way before you.... And *if you are willing to accept it, John himself is Elijah who was to come.*

Matthew 17:12-13

But *I say to you that Elijah already came,* and they did not recognize him, but did to him whatever they wished. So also the Son of Man is going to suffer at their hands. *Then the disciples understood that He had spoken to them about John the Baptist.*

To be sure, John did not come as Elijah the man, as Elijah the Tishbite. John came as Elijah in mission and message, that is, in spirit and in power. 5 So, since John was Elijah, the messenger of Malachi 3-4, then the message of John should be the message of Elijah; and indeed it was. John came preaching the judgment of Israel at the second coming of Christ in fulfillment of the great and terrible day of the Lord. The passage below encapsulates both the good news and bad news of John's message in fulfillment of Malachi's prophecy.

Matthew 3:1-2,7,9:

Now in those days John the Baptist came preaching in the wilderness of Judea, saying, Repent, for *the kingdom of heaven is at hand....* But when he saw many of the Pharisees and Sadducees coming for baptism, he said to them, *"You brood of vipers, who warned you to flee from the wrath to come?* 6 And do not suppose that you can say to yourselves, 'We have Abraham for our father'; for I say to you that from these stones God is able to raise up children to Abraham.... *The axe is already laid at the*

5. Mark 9:11-13 John 1:19-21
6. Some English translations such as the NASB render this phrase "the wrath to come". However, this is inaccurate. "Mello" is the Greek verb translated "to come" and it literally means, "of intention, to be about to do something" (Vines Expository Dictionary of New Testament Words). In other words, John is warning his audience of the wrath that is literally "about to" come upon them in their lifetime. This makes perfect sense seeing that both John and Jesus proclaimed that the kingdom was "at hand", and, that the kingdom and judgment (wrath) go hand in glove (Daniel 7, Isaiah 59, Matthew 16:27-28). If one was near, then so was the other. (Also see Luke 3:7-18, and specifically notice Luke's mention of "the gospel" in verse 18.) For John, the imminent "wrath" (judgment) that was about to come upon the unrighteous in fulfillment of Malachi 3-4 was considered good news. Only through judgment and separation by fire could the righteous of Israel inherit the kingdom. Thus, the gospel of the kingdom was both good and bad news for Israel.

root of the trees; therefore, every tree that does not bear good fruit is cut down and thrown into the fire. As for me, I baptize you with water for repentance, but He who is coming after me is mightier than I, and I am not fit to remove His sandals; He will baptize you with the Holy Spirit and fire. *His winnowing fork is in His hand, and He will thoroughly clear His threshing floor; and He will gather His wheat into the barn, but He will burn up the chaff 7 with unquenchable fire.*

This good news/bad news for Israel at the second coming of Christ is exactly what we saw earlier in our investigation of Isaiah 59 and Luke 21. Remember, it was only through Israel's "days of vengeance" 8 that her "day of salvation" 9 would come. But for John, this judgment was not something hundreds or thousands of years out in the future; it was imminent, it was "at hand," 10 it was a "wrath about to come".

This is important because as we have seen, John was primarily predicting the second coming of Christ, not his first (incarnation) coming. Therefore, unless John was completely confused about his mission and message, then the second coming of Christ in fulfillment of Malachi, was in fact *near* in the first century. In order to drive this point home, notice the imagery John uses to convey the

---

7. John's prediction that Christ's axe had been laid at the "*root* of the trees" and that at his coming he would "burn up the *chaff* with unquenchable fire", is a direct allusion to Malachi 4:1. Malachi said that at the coming of the Lord every evildoer will be *chaff*, and that the day of the Lord would set them *ablaze* leaving them neither *root* nor branch.
8. Deuteronomy 32:41-43, Isaiah 59:17-20, Isaiah 61:1-2, Luke 21:20-22. Although the theme of "vengeance" is not seen in the immediate context of Isaiah 62:11, it is present in the larger context of the prophecy. Isaiah 59, 61 and 63 all contain the element of vengeance. In Isaiah 59, vengeance is meted out at the coming of the Lord. All prophecies concerning the Lord's vengeance upon Israel were fulfilled by the fall of Jerusalem in AD70 (Luke 21:20-22,32).
9. Isaiah 63:4, Ephesians 4:30, Luke 21:28,32. According to Jesus, Israel's redemption was consummated through the destruction and judgment of Jerusalem in AD70.
10. Matthew 3:2. Not only was this the message of John the Baptist, it was the message of John the apostle in the book of Revelation. (22:6-12). When the apostle penned the Apocalypse, the Parousia of Jesus was to take place "soon", in fulfillment of Isaiah 40, Isaiah 62, and Matthew 16:27-28. For an in-depth word study on the Greek word "tachos" (translated "soon" in Revelation 1:1 and 22:6), see my article entitled, "Word Studies on Time Statements" parts one and two. These can be found on my website at www.reformedeschatology.com on the "Interpretation and Tools" page.

imminence of this judgment. An axe laid to the *root* of a tree insinuates that judgment has already begun. The root is now bare and exposed, and one final blow will sever the tree from its root completely, thus fully executing the judgment. Likewise, the winnowing fork in the hand of the Lord powerfully communicates that the *end* of the harvest was in view. These words of Jeremiah would have likely flooded their minds.

> Jeremiah 15:7
> *"I will winnow them with a winnowing fork* at the gates of the land; I will bereave them of children, *I will destroy My people...."*

One final thought concerning John's message of imminent judgment on Judah and Jerusalem. In Matthew 13 Jesus quotes both John and Malachi verbatim. The judgment of the wheat and the tares corresponds to the separation of the wheat from the chaff; and the binding and burning of the tares, refers to the burning of the evildoers as chaff. In his own interpretation of the parable, the judgment is called *the harvest*, and the harvest is the *end of the age.*

> Matthew 13:30,39-40
> Allow both to grow together until the harvest; and *in the time of the harvest* I will say to the reapers, *"First gather up the tares and bind them in bundles to burn them up; but gather the wheat into my barn.... the harvest is the end of the age....* 11

And undeniably, Jesus placed this *end-of-the-age-judgment* in the lifetime of his own generation. In other words, Jesus like John taught that the judgment of Israel at the second coming of the Lord in fulfillment of Malachi, was "at hand" in the first century. It was to occur at the fall of Jerusalem in AD70.

> Matthew 24:2-3,31,34
> And He said to them, "Do you not see all these things? Truly I say to you, *not one stone here will be left upon another, which will not be torn down."*
> As He was sitting on the Mount of Olives, the disciples came to Him privately, saying, "Tell us, *when will these things happen, and what will be the sign of Your coming, and of the end of the age?* ....And He will send forth

---

11. For anyone to suggest that the first century Jewish disciples connected the destruction of Jerusalem and the temple with the end of the "Christian age" and not the end of the Jewish age which that city and temple represented, is disturbing. According to the Hebrews writer, the removal of the Jewish temple would fully establish the New Covenant/Christian age (the time of reformation), not end it.

His angels with a great trumpet and they will gather together His elect…. Truly I say to you, *this generation will not pass away until all these things take place.*

Based on these connections between John, Jesus and Malachi, consider the following argument:

-Elijah the prophet would be sent to Israel to proclaim the second coming of Christ and the judgment of the day of the Lord, according to the word of Malachi.

-But, John was Elijah, who was sent to Israel and proclaimed the second coming of Christ, and the imminent judgment (the wrath about to come) of Jerusalem in fulfillment of the word of Malachi.

-Therefore, the second coming of Christ to judge and destroy Jerusalem at the great and terrible day of the Lord, was truly "at hand" in the first century.

And as always, this consistent testimony of scripture agrees perfectly with Matthew 16:27-28. Jesus said that his coming in his kingdom to repay "every man according to his deeds" was about to be accomplished in the lifetime of his contemporary disciples. John and Jesus both preached the same message; the gospel of the kingdom of God.

This means once again, that the coming of the Son of Man in his kingdom in Matthew 16:27-28 can't be limited to the reign of Christ at his ascension or to the birth of the church on Pentecost; but must be seen exactly for what it is: The full arrival of the rule and reign of Yahweh among Israel at the second coming of Messiah. John's identity as the messenger of Malachi to herald the imminent day of the Lord, is powerful biblical evidence that the second coming of Christ was in fact fulfilled in the generation to whom John was sent.

A CLOSER LOOK AT ISAIAH 40
THE GATHERING OF ISRAEL

Found within the context of Isaiah 40, is the great theme of the "gathering of Israel". According to Isaiah, this Messianic regathering would be accomplished at the return of Yahweh, that is, at the second coming of Christ.1 Let's read the text.

> Isaiah 40:10-11
> Behold, *the Lord God will come with might.... His reward is with Him....* Like a shepherd He will tend His flock, *in His arm He will gather the lambs....*

As we have seen with other themes/events in the bible, the gathering of Israel and the second coming of Christ are also synchronous events. Therefore, *the time* that the gathering of Israel takes place, is *the time* that the second coming of Christ must take place also. So, to determine the time of this last days 2 regathering, let's investigate a parallel prophecy which contains the same theme, spoken by the same prophet.

> Isaiah 11:12
> And He will lift up a standard for the nations and assemble the banished ones of Israel, *and will gather the dispersed of Judah from the four corners of the earth.*

And just to make it clear that we are dealing with truly parallel passages and not just similarity of language, notice that both texts mention a "highway" on which the Lord would gather Israel to himself.

---

1. As we have seen above, the return of Yahweh in Isaiah 40 was the message of John the Baptist. Clearly John interpreted this return of Yahweh as the second coming of Christ in salvation and judgment. (Matthew 3)
2. The writer of Hebrews makes it clear to his audience that they were living in the last days of the Old Covenant dispensation (1:1-2). Later in the letter, the writer urges his readers to not forsake their "assembling (gathering) together" as they saw "the day approaching" (10:25). In this context, this was clearly a "last days gathering" in anticipation of the return of the high priest from the MHP to consummate the day of atonement. (Hebrews 9:24-10:39) In 12:22   the writer says, "you have come to Mount Zion". The remnant of Israel was being gathered to the mountain of the Lord in fulfillment of Isaiah 2-4 in the first century, in Israel's last days.

Isaiah 40:3,11

".... Make smooth in the desert *a highway for our God*.... in His arm He will gather the lambs..."

Isaiah 11:12,16

"...And will gather the dispersed of Judah...." And *there will be a highway* from Assyria for the remnant of His people..."

Unless Isaiah prophesied two different highways for two different gatherings at two different returns of Yahweh to Zion, then what we are looking at is two parallel passages prophesying precisely the same event. The following comparative chart establishes the unity of these two prophecies....

ISAIAH 11-12	ISAIAH 40:1-11
Earth filled with the knowledge of the Lord (11:9)	Glory of the Lord revealed to all flesh (40:5)
The dispersed of Judah gathered (11:12)	The lambs of Judah gathered (40:9,11)
A spiritual highway (11:16)	A spiritual highway (40:3)
The return of the Lord to Zion (12:6)	The return of the Lord to Zion (40:9)
The salvation of Israel (12:2)	The salvation (reward) of Israel (40:10)

What this means of course is that the gathering of Israel in Isaiah 40 is the gathering of Israel in Isaiah 11. Therefore, *where ever* scripture places the gathering of Israel in Isaiah 11, that is where the gathering of Israel in Isaiah 40, (at the second coming of Christ), must be placed also. This being established, we will now investigate the larger context of Isaiah 11 in search of some answers. According to context, the gathering of Israel takes place *"in the day"* that....

1. The Spirit of the Lord rests upon Messiah, the Branch of Jesse (11:1-2)
2. The earth is full of the knowledge of the Lord. (11:9)
3. The nations resort to the Root of Jesse. (11:10)

As we shall see, the writers of the New Testament clearly place the fulfillment of each of these events/themes in the days of the first century, that is, in their generation. If this can be proven, it would be virtually impossible to deny that the gathering of Israel at the second coming of Christ in fulfillment of Isaiah 40, has not yet been fulfilled. I will do my best to keep my comments/arguments as succinct as possible.

Argument #1

-The gathering of Israel in Isaiah 11 would take place "in the day" that the Holy Spirit rested upon Jesus, the Branch of Jesse. (11:1-2)

78

-But, the Holy Spirit had rested (made its abode) upon Jesus in the first century, at his baptism in the Jordan....

> John 1:33
> "....*He upon whom you see the Spirit descending and remaining upon* Him, this is the One who baptizes in the Holy Spirit."

> Luke 4:18,21
> *The Spirit of the Lord is upon me....* And He began to say to them, "Today this Scripture has been fulfilled in your hearing." 3

-Therefore, Israel was being gathered in fulfillment of Isaiah 11 and Isaiah 40 in the first century, "in the day" that the Holy Spirit descended and rested upon Jesus at his baptism in the Jordan.

Argument#2
-The gathering of Israel in Isaiah 11 would take place "in the day" that the earth (the land) was full of the knowledge of the Lord. (11:9)

-But, through the preaching of the gospel in the first century, the knowledge of Christ (the Lord) had been made known to all nations and been heard "to the ends of the world", in fulfillment of the great commission.4

> Romans 16:25-26
> Now to Him who is able to establish you *according to my gospel and the preaching of Jesus Christ, according to the revelation of the mystery* which....now is manifested, and by the Scriptures of the prophets, according to the commandment of the eternal God, *has been made known to all the nations....*

---

3. In Luke 4 Jesus quoted Isaiah 61:1-2a and told the Jews of his day that "today (his day) this scripture is fulfilled in your hearing". Israel's restoration and release from bondage had begun through the ministry of Jesus. But, the restoration of Israel (the favorable day of the Lord) in Isaiah 61 was to take place at the "day of vengeance". This is not a contradiction, as we have seen, Jesus placed the climax of both the favorable day of the Lord (Israel's redemption - Luke 21:28) and the days of vengeance (Luke 21:22) at the coming of the Lord (Luke 21:27) in his contemporary generation (Luke 21:32).
4. The biblical fact is, the great commission commanded by Jesus was fulfilled in the first century. If this commission has not been fulfilled, then "the end of the (Jewish) age" has not yet come. (Matthew 24:2-3,14,34)

Romans 10:17-18
*So faith comes from hearing, and hearing by the word of Christ. But I say, surely
they have never heard, have they? Indeed they have; "Their voice has
gone out into all the earth, and the words to the ends of the world."*

Matthew 24:14,34
*This gospel of the kingdom shall be preached in the whole world as a testimony to
all the nations.... Truly I say to you, this generation will not pass away until
all these things take place.*

*-Therefore, Israel was being gathered in fulfillment of Isaiah 11 and Isaiah 40 in the first
century, "in the day" that the knowledge of the Lord through the gospel of Christ had been
made known to all nations throughout the whole Roman Empire (the "world").*

Argument #3
-The gathering of Israel in Isaiah 11 would take place "in the day" that the
nations (both Jew and Gentile) would resort (seek) to the Root of Jesse. (11:10)

-But, through the ministry of Paul and the apostles, the nations (both Jew and
Gentile) were seeking Jesus, the Root of Jesse, through faith in the gospel.

Romans 15:8-9,12
For I say that Christ has become a servant to the circumcision on behalf
of the truth of God *to confirm the promises given to the fathers, and for the
Gentiles to glorify God for His mercy; as it is written.... There shall come the
Root of Jesse, and he who arises to rule over the Gentiles, in Him shall the Gentiles
hope.* 5

*-Therefore, the gathering of Israel in fulfillment of Isaiah 11 and Isaiah 40 was taking place
in the first century, "in the day" that both Jew and Greek 6 began to seek Christ through the
gospel.*

It is more than evident that the writers of the New Testament taught that the
gathering of Israel in Isaiah 11, and by implication Isaiah 40, was being fulfilled

---

5.   Paul quotes Isaiah 11:10 verbatim in Romans 15:12 and directly applies it to
     his day. It is the opinion of the author that Isaiah 11:9 is also a primary Old
     Testament source for the doctrine of the great commission in the New
     Testament. For an excellent and compelling discussion of the first century
     fulfillment of the great commission see Don K. Preston's book, *"Into All The
     World Then Comes The End".*
6.   Romans 1:16, Amos 9:11-12, Acts 15:15-18

in their lifetime. Therefore, the second coming of Christ "in the day" of that gathering, in fulfillment of Isaiah, must have been "near" in the first century generation. Once again, this is exactly the message we find on the lips of the Messiah in his Olivet Discourse.

> Matthew 24:30-31,34
> And then the sign of the Son of Man will appear in the sky, and then all the tribes of the earth will mourn, and they will see *the Son of Man coming on the clouds of the sky* with power and great glory. And *He will send forth His angels with a great trumpet and they will gather together his elect* from the four winds, from one end of the sky to the other.... Truly I say to you, *this generation will not pass away until all these things take place.*

Not only do these words in Matthew vindicate a first century gathering of Israel at the second coming of Christ, they fulfill another great prophecy of the eschatological regathering of Israel in Isaiah chapter 27. 7

In the context of Isaiah 27, we see the return of Yahweh to judge Israel for shedding innocent blood, 8 and the *gathering together* of his elect at the sounding of the great trumpet. In Matthew 24, we see the Parousia (second coming) of Christ in judgment of Jerusalem for shedding innocent blood, 9 and the *gathering together* of his elect (the remnant of Israel) at the sound of the *great trumpet*. Perfect parallels, and Jesus places their fulfillment in his generation. 10

In conclusion, we have demonstrated that the coming of the Lord in Isaiah 40:10 was a prophetic source for the coming of the Son of Man in Matthew 16:27-28. We have also shown that the coming of the Lord in Isaiah 40 prophesied the covenant-return of Yahweh for the last day gathering of Israel in the first century. This means that Matthew 16:27-28 prophesied the second coming of Christ to gather together the elect in fulfillment of Isaiah 40, and must have been accomplished in the lifetime of Jesus' generation.

---

7. It is universally agreed that Matthew 24:31 is a direct quotation of Isaiah 27:12-13, an Old Testament prophecy of the eschatological gathering of Israel.
8. Isaiah 26:20-21
9. Matthew 21:33-45, 22:1-14, 23:29-24:2
10. Matthew 24:34

A CLOSER LOOK AT ISAIAH 62
THE MESSIANIC REMARRIAGE

As we have already shown, one of the primary Old Testament prophesies that Jesus drew from to predict his second and final coming in Matthew 16:27-28, was Isaiah 62:11. But remember, Jesus placed the time of that coming in the lifetime of his very first followers. What this means is, the coming of the Lord in Isaiah 62 must find fulfillment in Jesus' generation. We suggest that is exactly what scripture teaches. Much like Isaiah 40, we find a prominent eschatological theme within the context of Isaiah 62. That theme is, Yahweh's remarriage 1 to Israel.

The promise of the Messianic remarriage, was the promise of the return of the Lord to receive his bride to himself. He would give her a new name and establish her in righteousness; he would place her in a new Jerusalem and bless her under a New Covenant. Therefore, to determine *the time* of the wedding, will determine *the time* for the coming of the Lord for his bride, and thus, the second coming of Christ for the feast at the Messianic banquet. As has often been the case, we will begin by exploring the larger context of the prophecy.

In Isaiah 59:17-20, the Lord returns to Zion *clothed in righteousness and salvation* to establish the New Covenant with Israel. In the next chapter, Israel stands redeemed reflecting the glory of the Lord, *clothed in "garments of salvation" and wrapped with a "robe of righteousness"* (60:1-2,10). In other words, Israel has now put on the Lord's garments, he has clothed her in his likeness. As a matter of fact, this is exactly what we find in the following chapter....

---

1. The Lord had been a husband to all Israel, (Isaiah 54:5) but because of their harlotries, (Hosea 2:1-4, Jeremiah 3:1-8) the Lord had divorced and destroyed the northern kingdom. Yet in his mercy and faithfulness, he had promised to restore them through marriage under a new covenant (Hosea 2:14-23, Jeremiah 3:14-23). Thus, the marriage of Yahweh and Israel in Isaiah 62 would be the fulfillment of those promises. Following the divorce of the southern kingdom (Judah) in AD70, (Isaiah 65:1-15, Galatians 4:22-30, Matthew 21:33-45) Yahweh consummated his remarriage with "all Israel" as *one* nation and *one* kingdom under *one* King. Through the *Messianic remarriage*, the church has become the glorified bride of Christ (Revelation 21:1-11) in fulfillment of these promises made to Israel.

Isaiah 61:10
I will rejoice greatly in the Lord, my soul will exult in my God; for *He has clothed me with garments of salvation,* He has wrapped me with a robe of righteousness, *as a bridegroom decks himself with a garland, and as a bride adorns herself with her jewels.*

As a bride adorns herself with jewels, Isaiah sees the Lord adorning Israel. She is given His image and His glory 2 and becomes once again, the wife of Yahweh.

Isaiah 62:2-5
The nations will see your righteousness, and all kings your glory; and *you will be called by a new name which the mouth of the Lord will designate.* You will also be a crown of beauty in the hand of the Lord, and a royal diadem in the hand of your God. It will no longer be said to you, "Forsaken," nor to your land will it any longer be said, "Desolate"; but *you will be called, "My delight is in her," and your land, "Married". For the Lord delights in you, and to him your land will be married. For as a young man marries a virgin, so your sons will marry you; and as the bridegroom rejoices over the bride, so your God will rejoice over you.*

It is in this context that Yahweh comes (returns) to Zion with salvation. Isaiah prophesied the second coming of Christ to consummate the Messianic remarriage of Israel. Isaiah 62 is a recapitulation of the coming of the Lord in Isaiah 59.

Isaiah 62:11-12
Behold, the Lord has proclaimed to the end of the earth, say to the daughter of Zion, *"Lo, your salvation comes; behold His reward is with Him, and His recompense before Him."* And they will call them, "The holy people, the redeemed of the Lord"; and you will be called, "Sought out, a city not forsaken.

With this promise of Yahweh's remarriage to Israel in our hearts and minds, turn to the parables of Jesus, who in the plainest of speech and richest of imagery reveals *the time* that the Messianic wedding was be consummated. Jesus told a parable of a "King who gave a wedding feast for his Son", that he might confirm to Israel the promises made to their fathers. I say this in all sincerity; that only through the most reckless and torturous exegesis can the fulfillment of this

---

2. In Revelation 21:9f we see the church (the Lamb's wife) adorned in the glory of God, presented in the sight of all nations. *In and through his bride,* the glory of the Lord is forever present on earth, that "every eye" and "all flesh" may see.

prophecy be extended beyond AD70. As we'll see, even the staunchest of futurists tend to agree.

> Matthew 22:2-13
> The kingdom of heaven may be compared to *a king who gave a wedding feast for his son.* And he sent out his slaves to call those who had been invited to *the wedding feast,* and they were unwilling to come. Again, he sent out other slaves saying, 'Tell those who have been invited, "Behold, *I have prepared my dinner;* my oxen and my fattened livestock are all butchered and everything is ready; *come to the wedding feast."* But they paid no attention and went their way, one to his own farm, another to his business, and the rest seized his slaves and mistreated them and killed them. But *the king was enraged, and he sent his armies and destroyed those murderers and set their city on fire.* Then 3 he said to his slaves, *'The wedding is ready, but those who were invited were not worthy.* Go therefore to the main highways, and as many as you find there *invite to the wedding feast.* Those slaves went out into the streets and gathered together all they found, both evil and good; *and the wedding hall was filled with dinner guests.* But when the king came in to look over the dinner guests, *he saw a man there who was not dressed in wedding clothes,* and he said to him, 'Friend, how did you come in here without wedding clothes?' And the man was speechless. Then the king said to the servants, *'Bind him hand and foot, and throw him into the outer darkness; in that place there will be weeping and gnashing of teeth.*

In his commentary on this parable, the 19th century futurist commentator Matthew Henry says, "...*the scribes, and Pharisees, and chief priests; these were the*

---

3.   To suggest as some do, that "then" in verse 8 means that only *after* the destruction of Jerusalem by Rome was the invitation to the wedding feast extended to others outside of Jewry, is entirely foreign to the text. First of all, "then" (Gr. tote) does not mean "after", but "at that time". Second, Jesus does not teach that the call to the wedding was synchronous to the destruction of the murderers and the burning of their city. The call to the wedding was synchronous with the Lord's *sending forth of his armies to destroy* the murderers and burn their city. In other words, *at the time* when Israel had resolutely rejected   the invitation to their own wedding, that the Lord *then* (tote) sent forth his armies to destroy them. An example of this is seen in Jeremiah 51:11-12 where it says that the Lord "aroused the spirit of the kings of the Medes" to destroy Babylon. Significantly, the Lord did this "arousing" some 50 years before the Medes conquered Babylon. Similarly, the heavenly decree of the Lord *to send forth his armies* (the forces of Rome) to destroy Jerusalem, occurred decades before Rome surrounded the city in 67AD. While the Jews were rejecting the gospel, the Lord began to "arouse the spirit of the kings of the Romans".

persecutors, these took the servants, and treated them spitefully, and slew them.... the prophets and John the Baptist had been thus abused already, and the apostles and ministers of Christ must count upon the same." He continues, "The utter ruin that was coming upon the Jewish church and nation is here presented by the revenge which the king, in wrath, took on these insolent recusants (v.7); *He was wroth....* What was the ruin itself, that was coming; *He sent forth his armies.* The Roman armies were his armies, of his raising."4 (His emphasis)

Lang, seeing the connection between this parable and the promise of remarriage made to Israel says, "The Jews had long been want to think of the festival of the consummated kingdom of heaven under the figure of a feast". Quoting Isaiah 54:5 and Hosea 2:19-20 he goes on to say, "The change of the simple feast into a marriage supper rested upon the Old Testament representation of the covenant between Jehovah and Israel by the figure of the marriage state."5

Concerning the identity of them that were bidden (invited), David Brown says, "here meaning the Jews, who were "bidden", from the first choice of them onwards through every summons addressed to them by the prophets to hold themselves in readiness for the appearing of their King". And concerning the King's armies who burned up their city, Brown goes on to say, "The *Romans* are here styled as God's armies, just as the Assyrian is styled "the rod of His anger" (Isa 10:5), as being the executors of His judicial vengeance." 6 The Expositor's Greek Testament says, "... the allegory here evidently refers to the destruction of Jerusalem..."7

These futurist admissions of this parable are astonishing. Notice, this parable of Jesus finds fulfillment at the destruction of Jerusalem in AD70 (futurists agree). But the parable predicts the second coming of Christ to remarry Israel in fulfillment of Isaiah 62, at the time of that destruction. Therefore, the second coming of Christ to remarry the remnant of Israel took place at the destruction of

4. Matthew Henry, *Commentary In One Volume*, (Grand Rapids, Michigan; Zondervan Publishing), 1314
5. John Peter Lang, *A Commentary on the Holy Scriptures*, Sixth Section, 3rd Parable: The Marriage of the King's Son
6. Jamieson, Fausset, & Brown: Commentary on Matthew 22
7. *The Expositor's Greek Testament*, (New York; George H. Doran Company, 1897-1910), Matthew 22:7

Jerusalem in AD70. The parallels between Jesus and Isaiah in the context of the wedding are amazing!

Isaiah's prophecy depicts the righteous of Israel being clothed in salvation and righteousness 8 for the wedding, while those who did not turn from transgression in Jacob were slain and their "name" (identity) taken away. 9 Similarly, Jesus' parable depicts the righteous of Israel adorned in "wedding clothes" for the marriage, while those who had failed to prepare, were "cast out" from the presence of the King and excluded from the Messianic banquet.10 Old Covenant Israel had refused to prepare themselves for the wedding by putting on Christ. In the presence of the King, the clothes of the Old Covenant had always been "filthy garments." 11

In Luke 13, Jesus once again communicates the same message to Israel of his day. The wedding banquet - the "Messianic table"- would be made ready in their lifetime. The righteous would feast in the kingdom, yet those who had refused to enter through the narrow door of the gospel, would be cast out from the presence of the Lord.

> Luke 13:22-29
> And He was passing through from one city and village to another, teaching, and proceeding on His way to Jerusalem. And *someone said to him, "Lord, are there just a few who are being saved?"* And He said to them, "Strive to enter through the narrow door; for many, *I tell you, will seek to enter and will not be able.* Once the head of the house gets up and shuts the door, and you begin to stand outside and knock on the door, saying, 'Lord, open up to us!' then He will answer and say to you, 'I do not know where you are from. *Then you will begin to say, 'We ate and drank in Your presence, and You taught in our streets';* and He will say, 'I tell you, I do not know where you are from; depart from me, all you evildoers.' In that place, *there will be weeping and gnashing of teeth when you see Abraham and Isaac and Jacob and all the prophets in the kingdom of God, but yourselves being thrown out. And they will come from east and west and from north and south, and will recline at the table in the kingdom of God.*

There are several significant points we need to make concerning this passage. First, it was in response to a question concerning salvation that Jesus told this

---

8. Isaiah 61:10
9. Isaiah 65:15
10. Matthew 22:11-12, Matthew 8:10-12
11. Zechariah 3:1-4

parable of the wedding, the Messianic banquet. In other words, *Jesus connected salvation with the wedding.* This is no coincidence. As we have seen, Isaiah 62 also connects the salvation of Israel with the Messianic remarriage. Jesus is once again affirming and confirming the promises made to the fathers through the prophets.

Second, as with Jesus' parable in Matthew 21, the first century audience relevance in this text cannot be taken lightly. Notice what Jesus says concerning those who would fail to enter the door. They would stand outside say, *"We ate and drank in Your presence, and You taught in our streets".* The fact is, no one except the men of Jesus' contemporary generation could make these claims. More specifically, it was primarily, if not exclusively, first century Jews who had ate and drank in His presence and who he had taught in their streets.

Furthermore, Jesus specifically said to those same people, to his generation, "there will be weeping and gnashing of teeth *when you see* Abraham and Isaac and Jacob and all the prophets in the kingdom of God, but *yourselves being thrown out".* 12 It was the same generation of Jews that had dwelt (ate and drank) in his presence yet had rejected his gospel, that would be *cast out* from the kingdom of God. In a parallel passage, Jesus identified those same first century Jews as *"the sons of the kingdom".*

> Matthew 8:11-12
> I say to you that many will come from east and west, and *recline at the table* with Abraham, Isaac and Jacob in the kingdom of heaven; *but the sons of the kingdom will be cast out into the outer darkness; in that place there will be weeping and gnashing of teeth.*

Biblically speaking, this casting out of the "sons of the kingdom" cannot be a future-to-us event. If it is, then those of us in Christ (the sons of the kingdom) will

---

12. The Greek word translated as "thrown out" in Matthew 8:12 and Luke 13:28 is *ekballo*. It's the same word that Paul uses in Galatians 4:30 when he says, "cast out" *(ekballo)* the bondwoman and her son...". Paul and Jesus are speaking of the same casting out of Israel at the same time. In Galatians 5:5 Paul says, "For we through the Spirit, by faith, are waiting for *the hope of righteousness".* According to Isaiah 62, Israel would be clothed in *righteousness* at the coming of the Lord to consummate the marriage. Therefore, according to Paul, the marriage of Israel - *when she would put on righteousness* - would take place at the removal of the Old Covenant and the expulsion of the children which it produced. This took place at the destruction of the Old Covenant world in AD70.

one day be cast out. 13 This is an illogical and unbiblical position. The sons of the kingdom to which Jesus referred were Old Covenant Israel. The fact is, the generation which existed between 30-70AD was the first, the last, and *the only* generation in which *two covenant-bodies* of "kingdom-sons" existed simultaneously.

Through faith in Christ, the sons of the Old Covenant-kingdom, (the remnant of the natural lineage of Abraham, the body of Moses 14) were being transformed into sons of the New Covenant-kingdom (the spiritual seed of Abraham, the body of Christ). Yet for forty years, *both "sons of these kingdoms"* existed at the same time. 15 At the removal of Judaism in AD70, the sons of the old kingdom were *cast out*, and the *true* sons of the *true* kingdom, along with Abraham, Isaac, and Jacob, 16 sat down for the banquet at the Messianic remarriage of Israel. That was time when the saints took possession of the kingdom.

Having established the *time* of the wedding, we present the following thoughts concerning the *time* of the second coming of Christ, that is, the time of the coming of the bridegroom.

-The wedding takes place *when* Jerusalem is burned with fire (Matthew 22:1-14), when the sons of that kingdom are cast out (Matthew 8:11-12), and when the righteous are rewarded with the kingdom. (Matthew 8:11-12, 21:33-45)

-But Jerusalem was burned with fire (by Rome), the sons of that kingdom were cast out (Matthew 21:33-45 Matthew 22:1-14, Galatians 4:22-30), and the saints

---

13. This is precisely what the Dispensationalists teach. According to them, it is the church who is "cast out" from the presence of Jesus during the millennium. At that time, ethnic Israel enjoys 1000 years of blessings under a renewed Old Covenant economy. That is a horrid and evil doctrine.
14. 1 Corinthians 10:1-2,11 Hebrews 3:1-6 Jude 9.
15. See Galatians 4:21-31
16. According to the text, the wedding (Messianic banquet) feast represents the rewarding of the saints, when Abraham, Isaac, and Jacob are resurrected into the kingdom of God. But according to the text, the wedding feast takes place   at the destruction of Jerusalem (Matthew 22:1-14). Jesus was not preaching anything new. Both Daniel 12 and Revelation 11 teach that the rewarding of the saints takes place at the fall of Jerusalem in AD70; and, that *the rewarding of the saints was their resurrection into that kingdom.*

were rewarded with the kingdom, (Luke 21:31-32) at the end of the Old Covenant age in AD70. (Matthew 24:3,14,34)

-Therefore, the wedding feast took place at the end of the Old Covenant age in AD70, when Jerusalem was destroyed by fire, when the sons of the old kingdom were cast out, and when the saints were rewarded with the kingdom.

-But remember, the wedding feast takes place at the second coming of the Lord in fulfillment of Isaiah 62.

-Therefore, the second coming of Christ to remarry Israel in fulfillment of Isaiah 62, took place at the destruction of Jerusalem in AD70.

Once again, this is exactly what Jesus promised in Matthew 16:27-28. The second coming of Christ in fulfillment of Isaiah 62 was accomplished in the lifetime of Jesus' contemporary disciples; before all of those who were standing there had tasted death. And timewise, the destruction of Jerusalem in AD70 fits perfectly.

THE MARRIAGE AND THE MESSAGE OF JOHN

Any discussion of the return of the Lord for the remarriage of Israel in fulfillment of Isaiah 62, would be somewhat wanting without at least a brief interaction with the message of John the Baptist. I believe that John's message confirms what we have just set forth above; that the gathering of Israel at the second coming of Christ for the Messianic remarriage, was indeed *near* and therefore must have been *fulfilled* in the first century.

As we have seen, John was the "voice" of Isaiah 40 who came proclaiming that the salvation of Israel at the second coming of Christ was at hand. Yet, the salvation of Israel at the coming of Christ would be the time of Yahweh's remarriage to the remnant. This means that John came proclaiming that the Messianic remarriage of Israel in fulfillment of Isaiah 62, was "at hand" in the first century. As a matter of fact, through the message of the Baptizer we see the "historical fulfillment" 1 of one of Jesus' most explicit parables of the promised remarriage of Israel; the parable of the ten virgins.

> Matthew 25:1
> Then the kingdom of heaven will be comparable to *ten virgins,* who took their lamps and *went out to meet the bridegroom.*

Jesus did not give this parable as a timeless truth so that Christians of all generations would "be on the alert" 2 for the return of the bridegroom; not at all. The parable of the ten virgins was a "living parable", meant to illustrate what was currently taking place within Israel's last-days-story. That story, beginning with the preaching of John, was the coming again of the bridegroom for the wedding. This was, I suggest, the message of John the Baptist in Matthew chapter 3.

---

1. By "historical fulfillment" I mean then-ongoing fulfillment of Jesus' parable, beginning even prior to the time he spoke it. This was possible because many if not all of Jesus' parables were what N.T. Wright calls, "living parables". They revealed the then-present story and destiny of Israel that was at that time in *the process* of being "worked out". They invited Israel to take part in and embrace their own destiny. In this sense, Jesus' parables were not simply prophetic, but alive.

2. Many commentators such as Matthew Henry and Jamieson, Fausset & Brown understand it this way. This sort of self-application completely misses the message.

As we have seen, John came proclaiming the second coming of Christ to establish the kingdom *at the time of the remarriage of Israel* in fulfillment of Isaiah 62. Therefore, when Jerusalem, all Judea, and all the district around the Jordan *"went out"* to be baptized by John in obedience to his message and in expectation of its fulfillment, they were in reality, *"going out" to meet their bridegroom.* 3

> Matthew 3:1-6
> Now in those days John the Baptist came, preaching in the wilderness of Judea, saying, "Repent, for the kingdom of heaven is at hand." For *this is the one referred to by Isaiah the prophet when he said, "The voice of one crying in the wilderness, make ready the way of the Lord, make his paths straight"* Now John himself had a garment of camel's hair and a leather belt around his waist; and his food was locusts and wild honey. *Then Jerusalem was going out to him, and all Judea and all the district around the Jordan; and they were being baptized by him* in the Jordan River, as they confessed their sins.

In other words, Judah and "all the district around Jordan" represent the virgins 4 of Matthew 25. And just like the parable, so it was at the baptism of John. Not all who *"went out"* to meet the bridegroom responded with wisdom. As the parable says....

> Matthew 25:2
> "Five of them *were foolish,* and five were prudent."

The foolishness of the virgins was their rejection of the baptism of John, depending instead upon their natural lineage from Abraham. *"We have Abraham for our father"* was their shout of pride.

> Matthew 3:7-9
> "But when he saw many of the Pharisees and Sadducees coming for baptism, he said to them, "You brood of vipers, who warned you to flee from the wrath to come? Therefore, bear fruit in keeping with

---

3. John was not the bridegroom, but the "friend of the bridegroom" who testified of him. (John 3:26-20)
4. Israel is portrayed several times in the Old Testament as Yahweh's virgin (Jeremiah 18:13, 31:4,21 Lamentation 1:15, 2:13 Ezekiel 23:3,8 Amos 5:2). Although both kingdoms - the ten tribes in the north, and the two tribes in the south - became harlot wives (Hosea 2-5), it was the righteous remnant of all Israel that would once again constitute the one virgin bride of Yahweh under the New Covenant (2 Corinthians 11:2 Revelation 14:1-4, 21:2,9-11).

repentance; and *do not suppose that you can say to yourselves, 'We have Abraham for our father'..."*

This would prove to be a terrible mistake. To reject the message of John was to reject the call to the wedding. Those who would do so, would be excluded from the wedding of the Lord at his coming. However, those who had accepted John's message - the wise virgins - would become a "people prepared for the Lord."5

By submitting to the baptism of John the righteous remnant of Israel began the process of preparation and purification in anticipation of the coming of the bridegroom. The point is, John proclaimed that the Messianic remarriage of Israel in fulfillment of Isaiah 62 was *near* in the first century. Those who understood and accepted that message went out to meet the bridegroom, and were baptized. Understanding the message of John in the context of Isaiah 62 and the remarriage of Israel, has serious implications for the prophecy of Jesus in Matthew 16:27-28. 6 Consider the following argument:

- John preached the arrival of the Messianic kingdom at the second coming of Christ to remarry Israel, in fulfillment of Isaiah 62.

-But, the message of John was, "the kingdom of heaven *is at hand*".

-Therefore, the establishment of the Messianic kingdom at the second coming of Christ to remarry Israel in fulfillment of Isaiah 62, was in fact at hand in the first century.

This means that Matthew 16:27-28 means what it says, and says what is means; the coming of the Son of Man to establish his kingdom was the return of Christ to consummate his marriage with Israel in fulfillment of Isaiah 62, and was about to be accomplished in the lifetime of the first disciples. The second coming of Christ was the coming of bridegroom, when the bride received his name and image, and became partaker of his glory through marriage. 7

---

5. Luke 1:17, in fulfillment of Malachi 4:5-6. John came as the Elijah, and fulfilled the message of Malachi.
6. Once again, I am indebted to Don K. Preston for developing the connections which I draw upon here. I highly recommend Don's book, *"Elijah Has Come, A Solution to Romans 11:25-27"* where he develops these themes and connections much more in depth.
7. Revelation 21:9-11

PART II CONCLUSION

We have demonstrated that Daniel 7:13-14, Isaiah 59:17-21, Isaiah 40:10, and Isaiah 62:11 did in fact prophesy the second coming of Christ, and served as the major prophetic sources for Jesus' prophecy in Matthew 16:27-28.

We have demonstrated that the context and framework of Matthew 16 as well as these prophetic sources, make it is impossible to place the fulfillment of Matthew 16:27-28 at either Pentecost, the ascension, or the transfiguration events.

Finally, we have demonstrated conclusively that the major eschatological themes found within each of these Old Testament prophecies place the second coming of Christ in the lifetime of Jesus' contemporary generation, specifically, at the fall of Jerusalem in AD70.

In summary, Matthew 16:27-28 prophesied the second coming of Christ, in the glory of his Father, with his angels, and was fulfilled in the lifetime of his contemporary generation; at the fall of Jerusalem in AD70.

Below is one final chart which powerfully illustrates the evidence put forth so far through our investigation into the doctrine of the second coming of Christ.

MATTHEW 16:27-28	DANIEL 7	ISAIAH 59:17-21	ISAIAH 40:1-10	ISAIAH 62:1-11
Coming of the Son of Man (16:27)	Coming of the Son of Man (7:13,22)	Coming of the Redeemer (59:19-20)	Coming of the Lord (40:10)	Coming of the Lord (62:11)
Judgment of the Son of Man (16:27)	Judgment of the Son of Man (7:9,22)	Judgment of the Lord (59:18)	Judgment of the Lord (40:10)	Judgment of the Lord (62:11)
Coming in glory (16:27)	Coming in glory (7:9,14)	Coming in glory (59:19)	Coming in glory (40:5)	Coming in glory (62:2)
Coming with reward (16:27)	Coming with reward (7:18)	Coming with reward (59:18)	Coming with reward (40:10)	Coming with reward (62:11)
To establish the kingdom (16:28)	To establish the kingdom (7:14,22,27)	To establish the New Covenant (59:21)	To establish the kingdom (40:9-10)	To remarry Israel and establish the kingdom (62:1,2-5)
Fulfilled in the lifetime of Jesus' contemporary disciples FIRST CENTURY Matthew 16:28	Fulfilled in the "last days" (Daniel 2:28) -parallel text- FIRST CENTURY Hebrews 1:1-2	Fulfilled at the arrival of the New Covenant (59:17-18) FIRST CENTURY Hebrews 12:18-28	Fulfilled at the gathering together of Israel (40:9-11) FIRST CENTURY Matthew 24:31,34	Fulfilled at the Messianic remarriage of Israel (62:2-5) FIRST CENTURY Matthew 22:1-14

We believe to have made a thoroughly convincing case for the first century second coming of Christ primarily from the Old Testament prophetic sources of Matthew 16:27-28. We now turn our investigation towards the writings of the New Testament, where ironically for futurists, the prophecy that they deny, becomes *the source* for their future hope.

PART III

MATTHEW 16:27-28
A PRIMARY PROPHETIC SOURCE
FOR THE SECOND COMING
OF CHRIST
IN THE NEW TESTAMENT

STATING THE ARGUMENT

In Part II of this book we saw that Jesus, in Matthew 16:27-28 was quoting and confirming, yet at the same time radically redefining, some of the most anticipated and significant Old Testament prophecies concerning the Messianic hope of Israel through the covenant-return of Yahweh to his people. In other words, Matthew 16:27-28 prophesied the second coming of Christ in fulfillment of the prophets. In Part III now before us, we will demonstrate that in the New Testament, Matthew 16:27-28 becomes a primary prophetic source for the second coming of Christ as anticipated by the apostolic writers. But before we cite the prophecies which draw from Matthew 16:27-28, allow me to state our argument.

-Matthew 16:27-28 serves as a primary prophetic source for several significant prophesies in the New Testament.

-But, those significant prophesies in the New Testament prophesy the second coming of Christ.

-Therefore, Matthew 16:27-28 serves as a primary prophetic source for several significant "second coming prophesies" in the New Testament. Which means, Matthew 16:27-28 prophesied the second coming of Christ, and placed its fulfillment in the lifetime of Jesus' contemporary disciples.

Among others not explored in this work, Matthew 16:27-28 serves as the source and background for the following second coming prophesies in the New Testament.

1. Matthew 24:30-31 & 25:31
2. 1 Corinthians 15:51-54
3. 1 Thessalonians 4:15-17
4. 2 Thessalonians 1:4-10
5. 2 Timothy 4:1
6. Revelation 1:7
7. Revelation 22:12

So, to accomplish what we have set out to do - to establish the first century second coming of Christ - we must demonstrate definitively that all these texts do in fact prophesy the second coming of Christ, and, that Matthew 16:27-28 does in fact serve as their prophetic and eschatological source in what we call the New Testament. I hope you're still with me, this is about to get exciting!

MATTHEW 16:27-28 = REVELATION 22:12

In my opinion, what we are about to present below is some of the most definitive and compelling biblical evidence that Matthew 16:27-28 does refer to the second coming of Christ, and that it must have been fulfilled in the lifetime of the apostolic generation. 1 We now come face to face with its prophetic parallels in the New Testament, beginning in the book of Revelation. This following fact simply cannot be overemphasized: Matthew 16:27-28 serves as the primary New Testament prophetic source for the second coming of Christ as prophesied in the Apocalypse, specifically Revelation 22:12. 2 Let's begin by comparing the two passages from both the NASB and NIV.

> Matthew 16:27
> For *the Son of Man is going to come* in the glory of His Father with His angels, *and will then repay every man according to his deeds.*

> Revelation 22:12
> Behold, *I am coming quickly, and My reward is with Me, to render to every man according to what he has done.*

> Matthew 16:27 (NIV)
> For *the Son of Man is going to come* in his Father's glory with his angels, *and then he will reward each person according to what they have done.*

> Revelation 22:12 (NIV)
> Look, *I am coming soon!* My reward is with me, *and I will give to each person according to what they have done.*

Honestly, who can deny these parallels? John quoting Jesus, interprets the

---

1. By "apostolic generation" I mean Jesus' contemporary generation. The criteria for being an apostle of Christ is laid out in Acts 1:15-26 (compare this with Acts 10:36-43 and 13:30-33). Only one generation - the generation that walked, talked, drank and ate with Jesus - can be considered "apostolic". No *true* apostle of Christ has existed since then, nor ever will again.
2. It is hard to imagine how anyone could claim that Matthew 16:27-28 was fulfilled at either the transfiguration, the ascension or Pentecost, when the apostle John understood that very same text *to still be prophecy* more than thirty years after the fulfillment of those events. Furthermore, how can anyone deny that Matthew 16:27-28 prophesied the second coming of Christ when that is exactly how John applied it? It is neither arrogant nor presumptuous for proponents of covenant eschatology to challenge the futurist views of Matthew 16:27-28. In fact, it would be irresponsible for us not to.

coming of the Son of Man in Matthew 16:27-28 to be the second coming of Christ, that is, the eschatological revelation of Jesus. The implications of this are absolutely devastating for all futurist paradigms. Consider the following argument:

-Matthew 16:27-28 = Revelation 22:12

-But, Revelation 22:12 is a prophecy of the second coming of Christ.

-Therefore, Matthew 16:27-28 refers to the second coming of Christ as prophesied in Revelation 22:12, which Jesus promised to fulfill in the lifetime of his contemporary disciples.

In the face of this overwhelming evidence, it is hard to understand how anyone can miss - *or ignore* - that Matthew 16:27-28 lies behind the apostle John's prophesy of the second coming of Christ in Revelation 22. Yet many do, or so it seems. For example, A.R. Fausset sees Isaiah 40:10 and 62:11 as the prophetic source for Revelation 22:12, yet omits any mention of its obvious parallel to Matthew 16:27. 3 Likewise, G.K. Beale in his commentary of Revelation acknowledges that the coming of the Lord as promised in Isaiah 40 and 62 lies behind the coming of the Lord "quickly" in Revelation 22:12, yet mentions no connection whatsoever to Matthew 16:27-28. Beale goes so far as to say, "the emphasis is on Christ's future final return, as is shown by the promise, *"My reward is with Me, to render to every man according to what he has done,"* 4 but again fails to make any connection whatsoever to the identical phrase found in Matthew 16:28. How is this possible?

And notice the admission that Beale has made. Beale says, "the emphasis is on *Christ's future final return*, as is shown by the promise, *"My reward is with Me, to render to every man according to what he has done."* Ok, so if the words, "my reward is with me, to render to every man according to what he has done" in Revelation 22:12 refers to *"Christ's future final return"*, then the words, *"he will reward each person according to his works"* in Matthew 16:27 must also refer to *"Christ's future final return"*, as they are parallel passages. John was simply quoting Jesus, but more specifically, Jesus through his angel was confirming to John the immutability of his own promise. 5

---

3. Jamieson, Fausset and Brown: Commentary on Revelation 22 (BLB)
4. G.K. Beale, *Revelation A Shorter commentary*, (Grand Rapids, Michigan; Eerdmans, 2015), pp.516-517
5. Hebrews 6:16-18

Furthermore, Beale's suggestion that "quickly" means "speedily" rather than "soon in time", underscores his willingness to ignore the actual context of the passage as well as the obvious *"temporal parallel"* to Matthew 16:27-28. The phrase *"the time is near"* in Revelation 22:10 and *"some of those who are standing here who won't taste death until..."* in Matthew 16:28, provide the inspired interpretation of the word "quickly" in Revelation 22:12. The simple meaning is this: The appointed time was near for the prophecy of the book to be fulfilled, therefore the Lord was coming soon (quickly), even within the lifetime of some who had stood in his midst. Beale's complete silence regarding Matthew 16:27-28 in his discussion of Revelation 22:12 seems disingenuous to say the least.

Morris, like Fausset and Beale, also makes no mention of the connection between Revelation 22:12 and Matthew 16:27-28. 6 Neither does the Wycliffe Bible Commentary. In agreement with Beale, Wycliffe says concerning Revelation 12:22; "By quickly (v.12) is not meant that the Second Advent would occur soon after John completed the writing of this book. Rather, it means that the events of the Second Coming will occur so fast, one even quickly following another, that many will be taken completely by surprise." 7 At the risk of sounding repetitive, it is quite disturbing to me that well studied men such as these fail to *even mention* Matthew 16:27-28 in their discussions and exegesis of Revelation 22:12. Can we really assume that they haven't noticed the absolute perfect parallels listed on the following chart?

MATTHEW 16:27-28	REVELATION 22
Coming of the Son of Man (16:27)	Coming of Jesus (22:7,12,20)
To reward every man according to their works (16:27)	To reward every man according to their works (22:12)
To establish the kingdom (16:28)	To establish the New Jerusalem (22:14,19)
Fulfilled in the lifetime of Jesus' contemporary disciples (16:28)	Fulfilled "soon/shortly/quickly" (without delay, from when John wrote the book (22:6-7,10,12,20)

Not only are these texts similar in language, they are thematically identical. 8

---

6. Leon Morris, *Tyndale New Testament Commentaries, Revelation*, p.259
7. *The New Testament and Wycliffe Bible Commentary*, p.1105
8. Recall that Matthew 16:27-28 and its Old Testament prophetic sources - Daniel 7, Isaiah 40:1-10, 59:16-21, 62:1-11 - all followed the same thematic framework and pattern of persecution-judgment-vindication. The same is true for the larger context of Revelation 22:12 as well as many other New Testament prophesies which use Matthew 16:27-28 as their prophetic source.

Both texts concern judgment, reward, and the consummation of the kingdom. Furthermore, the judgment/reward theme in Revelation 22 fulfills the avenging/vindication of the martyrs anticipated in Revelation 6:9-11. Just like Matthew 16:27-28, the coming of Christ in Revelation 22:12 is to avenge his suffering saints and pass judgment on their persecutors; the framework of persecution-judgment-vindication is present once again.

Before we move on, consider one more thought concerning *time* in Revelation 22. By the time John wrote Revelation, 9 many of the disciples who had heard Jesus' words in Matthew 16:27-28 would have already "tasted death". Therefore, if his promise was to be kept and his prophecy fulfilled, *on time*, then his coming had to take place "soon" from the time that John wrote. For John, *soon* did not mean thousands of years off. *Soon meant John's generation,* 10 *in fulfillment of Jesus' prophecy.* The reason why Jesus through his angel instructed John to write, "behold I am coming quickly, and my reward is with me…" is because that was exactly what Jesus had promised would take place more than three decades earlier; *"…some of those who are standing here won't taste death until they see the Son of Man coming…".* The time was near for the prophesies of both Jesus and John to be fulfilled. Therefore, John was told, "do not seal up the words…" as there would be no more delay. 11

---

9. The author takes the early date position, approximately AD64-66AD.
10. Many attempt to twist and distort the plain and consistent meaning of the Greek words "tachos, tachy and eggys", translated as "soon, quickly and near" in verses 6,7,10,12,20 of chapter 22 to mean, "thousands of years away". This is obviously nothing more than a desperate tactic to maintain a futurist eschatology at all costs. For a thorough refutation of these futurist attempts, see my four-part study entitled "Word Studies on Time Statements" on my website, www.reformedeschatology.com. I investigate the use of these words throughout the book of Revelation as well as the rest of the New Testament and demonstrate that they are *always* used in a first century context.
11. It is strange, to say the least, that commentators see the contrast between Revelation 22:10, "do not seal up the words…. for the time is near", and Daniel 8:26, "keep the vision secret, for it pertains to many days in the future", as well as Daniel 12:4, "conceal these words and seal up the book until the end of time"; *yet fail to honor the time element being contrasted.* Daniel's "many days" and "end of time" (better translated as "time of the end") *did mean* a long time off from Daniel's days. But, we are told that John's "the time is near" *did not mean* soon from John's day. G.K. Beale is guilty of this inconsistency, (*Revelation A Shorter Commentary*, pp.512-513). See Don K. Preston's book, *"Who Is This Babylon"* for an in-depth analysis on the contrast between the prophesies of John and Daniel concerning *time.*

In conclusion; what we have seen is clear and undeniable biblical testimony that refutes all futurist paradigms which place the second coming of Christ beyond the lifetime of Jesus' generation. Matthew 16:27-28 served as the New Testament prophetic source for Revelation 22:12. But Revelation 22:12 prophesied the "soon" and "at hand" second coming of Christ. Therefore, Matthew 16:27-28 prophesied the second coming of Christ, and in agreement with John, limited its fulfillment to the lifetime of Jesus' generation.

A CLOSER LOOK AT REVELATION 22:12
THE GREAT WHITE THRONE JUDGMENT

John's words, *"to reward every man according to his works"* in Revelation 22:12 takes on even greater significance when interpreted through the larger context of the passage. Twice in chapter 20 John uses the exact same phrase that he does in Revelation 22:12, but in the former, it's used in the context of the millennium resurrection. This is important. Here are the two passages, one after another....

> Revelation 20:11-13
> Then I saw a great white throne and Him who sat upon it, from whose presence earth and heaven fled away, and no place was found for them. And *I saw the dead, the great and the small, standing before the throne, and books were opened;* and another book was opened, which is the book of life; and *the dead were judged from the things which were written in the books, according to their deeds.* And the sea gave up the dead which were in it, and death and Hades gave up the dead which were in them; and *they were judged, every one of them according to their deeds.*

> Revelation 22:12
> Behold, I am coming quickly, and My reward is with Me, *to render to every man according to what he has done.*

What this means is that the coming of the Lord in Revelation 22:12 was his coming at the end of the millennium resurrection in Revelation 20, to judge *"every one of them according to their deeds"*. Said another way, the end of the millennium resurrection (20:5f) would be accomplished at the coming of the Lord in Revelation 22:12 to *"render to every man according to what he has done"*. But remember, Matthew 16:27-28 is the source for Revelation 22:12, they are parallel passages. These being the facts, consider the following argument:

-The coming of the Son of Man in Matthew 16:27-28 = the coming of Christ in Revelation 22:12

-But, the coming of Christ in Revelation 22:12 takes place *at the end of the millennium resurrection* to execute "the judgment", and therefore *must* refer to the second coming of Christ.

-Therefore, the second coming of Christ at the end of the millennium resurrection to execute "the judgment" in Revelation 22:12, would be in fulfillment of the coming of the Son of Man in Matthew 16:27-28.

-But remember, the coming of the Son of Man in Matthew 16:27-28 was fulfilled in the lifetime of Jesus' contemporary disciples.

-Therefore, the second coming of Christ at the end of the millennium resurrection to execute "the judgment" in Revelation 22:12, would be in fulfillment of the coming of the Son of Man in Matthew 16:27-28, and was accomplished in the lifetime of Jesus' contemporary disciples.

If we are going to take seriously the inspiration of scripture and honor the words of Jesus and his apostles, then there remains only one conclusion: It was the first century generation who experienced "the end of all things", 1 when all things that had been written were fulfilled. 2

---

1.   1 Peter 4:7
2.   Luke 21:22

MATTHEW 16:27-28 = REVELATION 1:7

The second passage we will investigate is Revelation 1:7. No matter their eschatological persuasion, commentators have long realized, and rightly so, that the Old Testament prophetic source for Revelation 1:7 is primarily two-fold: Daniel 7:13 and Zechariah 12:10. 1 Commentators have also   correctly understood the coming of the Lord in Revelation 1:7 to be his coming in vindicatory-judgment. In other words, his coming is to avenge the blood of the saints. For example, concerning Revelation 1:7 Morris says, "Their overthrow means the triumph of good and the vindication of Christians who had suffered so much." 2 However, admissions such as these deal a death blow to all futurist eschatology's. Notice the implication of the prophecy/fulfillment relationship between Revelation 1 and Daniel 7.

-Revelation 1:7 = Daniel 7:13 - an Old Testament prophecy of the second coming of Christ to judge the persecutors of the saints, fulfilled in AD70.
-But, Daniel 7:13 = Matthew 16:27-28 - a New Testament prophecy of the second coming of Christ to judge the persecutors of the saints, fulfilled in AD70.
-Therefore, Revelation 1:7 is a prophecy of the second coming of Christ to judge the persecutors of the saints in fulfillment of Daniel 7:13 and Matthew 16:27-28, which were fulfilled in AD70.

There are two points that need to be made at this juncture. First, this conclusion agrees perfectly with what we have shown above concerning *time* in Revelation 22. Both Revelation 1:7 and Revelation 22:6-12, which are in fact "book-end prophesies", 3 place the second coming of Christ in the first century. Second, if Daniel 7:13 serves as a prophetic source for Revelation 1:7, yet Revelation 1:7 was still prophecy in John's day, then Daniel 7 could not possibly have been fulfilled at the ascension of Jesus. This vindicates our earlier investigation of

---

1. For example, see *"Revelation A Shorter Commentary"*, G.K. Beale, pp.42-43, and *"Tyndale New Testament Commentaries, Revelation"*, Leon Morris, pp.49-50. In his commentary, Beale fails to explain how he sees Revelation 1:7 as a prophecy future to John in his day, yet at the same time sees Daniel 7:13 (the prophetic source for Revelation 1:7) fulfilled at the ascension of Christ. It is simply impossible to have it both ways.
2. Leon Morris, *Tyndale New Testament Commentaries, Revelation*, p.50.
3. Compare Revelation 1:1-3,7 with Revelation 22:6-12. These parallel time-limited prophesies form a powerful "inclusio" in which the entire book must be viewed and interpreted. The message being communicated was that the "time was near" for everything prophesied in the book to "soon take place".

Daniel 7. But let's move on. As just mentioned, Revelation 1:7 is a direct quote from Zechariah 12:10. But, the application of Zechariah's prophecy by the apostle John also limits the fulfillment of Revelation 1:7 to the first century. Below are the two texts.

> Zechariah 12:10
> "...they will look on Me whom they have pierced; and they will mourn for Him, as one mourns for an only son..."

> Revelation 1:7
> 'Behold he is coming with the clouds, and every eye will see Him, even those who pierced Him; and all the tribes of the earth will mourn over Him..."

Notice specifically the phrase, "they will look on Me whom they have pierced". John tells us in his gospel that this portion of Zechariah's prophecy was fulfilled at the cross of Christ, when those who pierced him looked upon him.

> John 19:36-37
> For these things came to pass to fulfill the Scripture, "Not a bone of Him shall be broken." And again, another Scripture says, "They shall look on him whom they pierced."

According to John, those who had looked on him when they pierced him, would see him coming with the clouds. 4 But those who looked on him when they pierced him were first century Jews. 5 Therefore, those first century Jews who had pierced him would see him coming with the clouds. This means that Revelation

---

4. See Don K. Preston's book, "Like Father Like Son on Clouds of Glory" for the most compelling study on the "cloud-coming" of Jesus available. In the ancient world, "coming with the clouds" was a powerful Hebrew metaphor for both deity and judgment. Concerning this phrase in the context of Jerusalem's destruction in Mark 13, N.T. Wright says, "The disciples now "heard" his prophetic announcement of the destruction of the Temple as the announcement, also, of his own vindication; in other words, of his own "coming" - not floating around on a cloud, of course, but of his "coming" to Jerusalem as the vindicated, rightful king."

5. Acts 2:36, 3:14-17, 1 Corinthians 2:6-8, Matthew 27:39-43, Mark 15:29-32, Luke 23:35-48 John 19:36-37. Although it was a Roman spear that pierced the side of Jesus, it was the Jews of his generation - according to their own request (Matthew 27:22-25) - who were held guilty of his murder. It is in this manner that the Jews of his day had pierced him. The fact that the very Jews responsible for the death of their Messiah looked upon him on the cross, limits both Zechariah 12:10 and Revelation 1:7 to a first century fulfillment.

1:7 - the coming of Christ in judgment - must have been fulfilled in the lifetime of the Jews who pierced him 6 in fulfillment of Zechariah 12:10.7 The truth is, this is precisely what Jesus had promised more three decades earlier. On the eve of his crucifixion Jesus prophesied to the Jews who were *about to pierce him,* that *they* would once again *see him*…. coming with the clouds.

---

6. Logically, if those who looked on him when they pierced him were to see him coming with the clouds, then his coming with the clouds must have taken place in the lifetime of those who pierced him. Since those who pierced him were first century Jews, then his coming with the clouds must have occurred in the lifetime of those first century Jews.
7. This agrees perfectly with the *time frame* given for the fulfillment of Zechariah's prophecy. The great mourning would be in Jerusalem and Judah (Zechariah 12:2,10-12). It would be when "the Spirit of grace and supplication" was poured out upon the house of David and the inhabitants of Jerusalem (Zechariah 12:10). This began to be fulfilled on the day of Pentecost (Acts 2).

A CLOSER LOOK AT REVELATION 1:7
MATTHEW 26:64 & MORE

While commentators are quick on the trigger to point out the connection between Revelation 1:7 and passages such as Daniel 7 and Zechariah 12:10, they seem slow on the draw to make the connection between Revelation 1:7 and Matthew 26:64. Yet the connection is valid, and extremely important. For example, notice the parallels between Jesus' words to the religious leaders who were about to *pierce him*, and John's words in Revelation.

> Matthew 26:64
> *".... you will see the Son of Man* sitting on the right hand of power, and *coming on the clouds of heaven."*

> Revelation 1:7
> *".... he is coming with the clouds, and every eye will see Him, even those who pierced Him...."*

It was the first century Jews who pierced Jesus, therefore, Revelation 1:7 must be understood as the fulfillment of Matthew 26:64. Jesus told Caiaphas that that *they* 1 would see him "coming on the clouds" in judgment against them. John said that those who pierced Jesus would *see* him "coming with the clouds" in judgment of them; *soon*. Therefore, the Jewish generation who had "killed the Prince of Life" 2 was judged and destroyed at the coming of the Son of Man in AD70, in fulfillment of Revelation 1:7 and Matthew 26:64.

What should not be overlooked in all of this is that Psalms 110 along with Daniel 7 serve as prophetic sources for Matthew 26:64. I will do my best to explain the significance. Jesus' conflation of Psalms 110:1 *"sitting on the right hand of power"* and Daniel 7:13 *"coming on the clouds of heaven"* in Matthew 26:64, serves as a powerful interpreter for the *context* 3 of the coming of the Son of Man. I suggest that the coming of the Son of Man in Matthew 26:64 refers to the return of Christ from

---

1. When Jesus answers Caiaphas, "... *you* will see the Son of Man...", he is at the very least referring to the body of the Sanhedrin, not Caiaphas alone. In the Greek, *"you"* is in the plural form, not the singular. However, I personally believe that Jesus' *"you"* referred not just to the body of the Sanhedrin, but to the *entire body* of the unbelieving Jewish nation, which Caiaphas and the Sanhedrin ruled and *represented.*
2. Acts 3:15
3. By *context* I mean the "time, nature, and purpose".

108

the right hand of the Father in Zion, to place all enemies under his feet and to shatter kings and chief men "in the day of his wrath". 4

In other words, the coming of the Son of Man in Matthew 26:64 refers to the second coming of Christ to exercise the sovereignty of his kingdom and the subjugation of his enemies, in fulfillment of Psalms 110 and Daniel 7. 5 And, since Matthew 26:64 parallels Revelation 1:7, and Revelation 1:7 parallels Matthew 16:27-28, then the coming of the Son of Man in Matthew 16:27-28 refers to the second coming of Christ in AD70 - *in the lifetime of those who pierced him* - in fulfillment of Psalms 110, Daniel 7 and of course Matthew 26:64.

But that's not all, Jesus' prophecy in Matthew 24:30 also stands behind the cloud-coming of Christ in John's Apocalypse. For the most part commentators acknowledge this, yet for whatever reason, some fail to document it. 6 Below are some parallels between Revelation 1:7 and Matthew 24:30 followed by a comparative chart, illustrating that what Jesus had prophesied in the 30's, John prophesied in the 60's, and that *both* placed the fulfillment of their prophecies in that *same generation*.

> Revelation 1:7
> Behold, *he is coming with the clouds, and every eye will see Him,* even those who pierced Him; *and all the tribes of the earth will mourn over Him.* So it is to be. Amen.

---

4. Psalms 110:5
5. In fulfillment of Psalms 2 as well; Psalms 2 and Psalms 110 being parallel prophesies. Also, consider how this understanding of the "coming of the Son of Man" affects the futurist interpretation in Daniel 7. If the coming of the Son of Man in Daniel 7 refers to the coming of Christ out of Zion in fulfillment of Psalms 2 and 110, then Daniel 7 cannot possibly find fulfillment at the transfiguration, the ascension, or any event pre-AD70.
6. Strangely, G.K. Beale makes no connection whatsoever between Revelation 1:7 and Matthew 24:30 in his commentary. *"Revelation, A Shorter Commentary"*. Neither does Leon Morris (*Tyndale New Testament Commentaries*, Revelation, 2015). Although Morris does connect Revelation 1:7 with Revelation 22:20, (p.49) he fails to see, or at least document, the implications of this connection. The "coming" of Revelation 22:20 is the "coming" of Revelation 22:12. But the coming of 22:12 is the coming of Matthew 16:27-28 which was fulfilled in Jesus' generation. Therefore, Revelation 1:7 and Revelation 22:20 prophesied the second coming of Christ and was fulfilled in the lifetime of Jesus' first disciples.

Matthew 24:30 (NKJV)
Then the sign of the Son of Man will appear in heaven, and then *all the tribes of the earth will mourn, and they will see the Son of Man coming on the clouds of heaven* with power and great glory.

MATTHEW 24:30	REVELATION 1:7
The coming of the Son of Man	The coming of Jesus
On the clouds	With the clouds
All tribes of the earth will see Him	Every eye will see Him
All tribes of the earth will mourn	All tribes of the earth will mourn
Fulfilled in the lifetime of Jesus' first century generation (24:34)	Fulfilled when those who pierced him (first century Jews) would see him, the time was near

The apostle obviously had Jesus' Olivet discourse in mind. But more accurately, and as we have already mentioned, Jesus by his angel was signifying to John what he had personally told him several decades earlier. The "promise of his coming" had not failed as the scoffers had assumed; the day of the Lord and the judgment of that day was truly about to be accomplished. Therefore, consider the following argument:

-The coming of the Son of Man in Revelation 1:7 = the coming of the Son of Man in Matthew 24:30. (see chart above)

-But, the coming of the Son of Man in Matthew 24:30 = the coming of the Son of Man in Matthew 16:27-28 which was fulfilled in the lifetime of Jesus' contemporary disciples. (see chart below)

MATTHEW 16:27-28	MATTHEW 24:30-31
Coming of the Son of Man (16:27-28)	Coming of the Son of man (24:30)
His coming in glory (16:27)	His Coming in glory (24:30)
With the angels (16:27)	With the angels (24:31)
Judgment of all men (16:27)	All tribes of the earth will mourn, gather together the elect (24:30)
To establish the kingdom (16:28)	To establish the kingdom (Luke 21:31 – parallel prophecy)
Fulfilled in the lifetime of Jesus' disciples (16:28)	Fulfilled in the lifetime of Jesus' first century generation (24:34)

-*Therefore, the coming of the Son of Man in Revelation 1:7 was fulfilled in the lifetime of Jesus' contemporary disciples, in fulfillment of Matthew 16:27-28.*

But notice what this means....

-The coming of the Son of Man in Revelation 1:7 was fulfilled in the lifetime of Jesus' contemporary disciples, in fulfillment of Matthew 16:27-28.

-But, the coming of the Son of Man in Matthew 16:27-28 = the second coming of Christ in Revelation 22:12. (see chart below)

MATTHEW 16:27-28	REVELATION 22
Coming of the Son of Man (16:27)	Coming of Jesus (22:7,12,20)
To reward every man according to his works (16:27)	To reward every man according to his works (22:12)
To establish the kingdom (16:28)	To establish the New Jerusalem (22:14,19)
To be fulfilled in the lifetime of Jesus' contemporary disciples (16:28)	To be fulfilled "soon/shortly/quickly" from when John wrote (22:6-7,10,12,20)

-Therefore, the coming of the Son of man in Revelation 1:7 was the second coming of Christ in fulfillment of Matthew 16:27-28, and was accomplished in the lifetime of Jesus' contemporary disciples, through the judgment of those who pierced him, just as the text demands.

In conclusion, we have shown clearly and consistently that Matthew 16:27-28 served as prophetic source for *two* of the most explicit and undeniable second coming prophesies in all the New Testament, (Revelation 1:7 and 22:12), and placed their fulfillment within the lifetime of Jesus' disciples. Therefore, it remains an undeniable fact; Matthew 16:27-28 prophesied the second coming Christ, which did find fulfillment in the generation of Jesus Christ.

MATTHEW 16:27-28 = MATTHEW 24 & 25
THE OLIVET DISCOURSE

The next passage we will investigate is Jesus' famous Olivet discourse. But before we begin, we simply make mention the fact that many futurists see a "separation" within this great prophesy. Although futurist camps are divided (pun intended) as to where the discourse should be separated, most will agree that a "gap" of nearly 2000 years must be inserted *somewhere* within the text. In other words, futurism sees some parts of the prophecy fulfilled in the fall of Jerusalem in AD70 and earlier; and other parts not yet fulfilled, even until this day. But as we shall show, this position is entirely untenable and can be dismissed with little effort. Matthew 24 and 25 constitute one continuous prophecy foretelling the second coming of Christ in fulfillment of Matthew 16:27-28, as well as numerous Old Testament prophecies.

As we begin, notice how several commentators have interpreted the judgment-coming of the Son of Man in Matthew 25:31f. Lang says, "He exercises judgment now upon all the nations of the earth, and upon all the generations of men.... *His sentence introduces a separation which must bring the earth itself, in its ancient form, to an end*; for, the good are received into the kingdom of the Father, and the wicked are cast into hell."1 Guzik says, "it is a description of a future scene of judgment *after the glorious second coming of Jesus* (described in Matthew 24:30)". 2 Ice says the text is, "a key New Testament passage that includes the sheep and goat judgment *after the second coming.*" 3

These men clearly interpret Matthew 25:31f to be the last-day judgment following the second coming of Christ. Yet as usual, these futurist admissions are destructive to their own positions. The following chart illustrates that Matthew 24 and 25 cannot be divided, but together, form one united prophecy concerning the judgment of the Jewish nation, the end of the Jewish age, and the Parousia of Christ in "this (the first century) generation". Notice the absolute perfect parallels....

---

1. Lange, *Commentary on Holy Scriptures*, Fifth Section, (Matthew 25:31-46)
2. David Guzik, *Study Guide for Matthew 25*, BLB
3. Thomas Ice, *An Interpretation of Matthew 24-25*, BLB

MATTHEW 24:30-34	MATTHEW 25:31-34
Coming of the Son of Man (24:30)	Coming of the Son of Man (25:31)
Coming in glory (24:30)	Coming in glory (25:31)
With his angels (24:31)	With his angels (25:31)
Gathering of the elect (24:31)	Gathering of the sheep (25:32-33)
Establishment of the kingdom (Luke 21:31 - parallel prophecy)	Establishment of the kingdom (25:34)
Fulfilled in Jesus' generation, at the end of the age (24:3,34)	Fulfilled when the righteous (the sheep) inherit the kingdom (25:35)

Clearly, the coming of the Son of Man - in glory, with the angels - in Matthew 24 and 25 are parallel prophesies concerning same-time events, and therefore interpret each other. For example, the Son of Man *coming* to gather together *his elect*, is equivalent to the Son of Man *coming* to give *the sheep* their inheritance; a beautiful picture of the saints receiving the kingdom at the second coming of Christ. 4 Simply stated, the judgment scene in Matthew 25 illustrates what took place at Christ's end of the age Parousia in Matthew 24. Based on these parallels, consider the implications for futurists who see Matthew 25:31f as a prophecy of the "glorious second coming of Jesus".

-The coming of the Son of Man in Matthew 25:31f prophesied the second coming of Christ (many futurists agree).

-But, the coming of the Son of Man in Matthew 25:31f = the coming of the Son of Man in Matthew 24:30-31 which was fulfilled in Jesus' generation (24:34)

-Therefore, the coming of the Son of Man in both Matthew 24:30-31 and 25:31f prophesied the same second coming of Christ which was fulfilled in Jesus' generation.

But, if the coming of the Son of Man - in glory, with his angels - in both Matthew 24 and 25 refers to the second coming of Christ, then what are we to make of the coming of the Son of Man - in glory, with his angels - in Matthew 16:27- 28? Was Jesus prophesying two separate "comings" to be fulfilled at two very separate times? Some futurists think so. I believe the following chart provides us with the biblical answer....

---

4.   This is the identical framework that we saw in Matthew 16:27-28 Daniel 7, Isaiah 40, 59, and 62. The coming of the Lord is in both judgment and reward, to establish the kingdom. The Olivet discourse is yet another example of Jesus confirming the promises made to the fathers of Israel. (Romans 15:8) We will see this framework again as we continue our investigation.

MATTHEW 16:27-28	MATTHEW 24:30-31	MATTHEW 25:31f
Coming of the Son of Man (16:27-28)	The coming of the Son of man (24:30)	Coming of the Son of Man (25:31)
His coming in glory (16:27)	His Coming in glory (24:30)	His coming in glory (25:31)
With the angels (16:27)	With the angels (24:31)	With the angels (25:31)
Judgment of all men (16:27)	All tribes of the earth will mourn, gather together the elect (24:30)	Judgment of all nations (25:32)
To establish the kingdom (16:28)	To establish the kingdom (Luke 21:3 - parallel text)	To establish the kingdom (25:34)
Fulfilled in the lifetime of Jesus' disciples (16:28)	Fulfilled in Jesus' first century generation (24:34)	Fulfilled when the righteous inherit the kingdom (25:34) (1st century - Luke 21:31)

There is no sense in trying to deny the obvious. Jesus' promise in Matthew 16 was without a doubt the background for his prophecy in his united Olivet discourse. At least twice during his ministry, Jesus publicly proclaimed that his glorious coming in judgment, with his angels, to establish his kingdom, was about to be accomplished in the lifetime of his contemporary disciples.

Author Gary DeMar, although not a preterist, gives an honest assessment of these connections when he says, *"There is little evidence* that the "coming of the Son of Man" in Matthew 24:27,30,39 and 42 is different from the coming of the Son of Man in Matthew 25:31. Compare Matthew 25:31 with 16:27, a certain reference to the destruction of Jerusalem in AD70... These verses are almost identical." 5 Although DeMar's logic is sound and his honesty commendable, I doubt that he realized the full implication of his statement. Based on the foregoing charts which agree with DeMar's statement, consider the following argument:

-The coming of the Son of Man in Matthew 25:31f prophesied the second coming of Christ (many futurists agree).
-But, the coming of the Son of Man in Matthew 24:30-31, Matthew 25:31f, and Matthew 16:27-28 all prophesied the destruction of Jerusalem in AD70 (Gary DeMar).
-*Therefore, the second coming of Christ was fulfilled at the destruction of Jerusalem in AD70 as prophesied in Matthew 16:27-28, Matthew 24:30-31, and Matthew 25:31.*

---

5. Gary DeMar, *Last Days Madness: Obsession of the Modern Church,* (Powder Springs; American Vision, 4th edition., 1999), p.200

The biblical evidence demands that the entirety of the Olivet discourse (Matthew 24-25) be interpreted as *one* indivisible prophecy, consummating in the fall of Jerusalem and the second coming of Christ in AD70, in fulfillment of Matthew 16:27-28.

A CLOSER LOOK AT THE OLIVET DISCOURSE
THE GREAT TRUMPET OF GOD

According to Jesus, the coming of the Son of Man and the sounding of the "great trumpet" were to be synchronous (same time) events. This undeniable fact further establishes that the Olivet discourse did prophesy the second coming of Christ at the end of the Jewish age in AD70. But more than that, the great trumpet of God marks the time of the great resurrection of Israel; when their dead would live, and their corpses would rise again. Let's look a bit closer....

It is widely accepted even by the premillennialists, that Jesus' reference to the "great trumpet" within the Olivet Discourse was a direct allusion to Isaiah 27:13. For example, Arnold Fruchtenbaum says, "In the New Testament, the *final regathering* revealed by the Old Testament prophets is summarized in Matthew 24:31 and Mark 13:27.... The Matthew passage is based on Isaiah 27:12-13...." [1] We could not agree more, after all, the parallels speak for themselves....

> Isaiah 27:13
> It will come about also in that day that *a great trumpet will be blown,* and those who were perishing in the land of Assyria and *who were scattered in the land of Egypt* will come and worship the Lord in the holy mountain at Jerusalem.

> Matthew 24:31
> And He will send forth His angels *with a great trumpet and they will gather together His elect from the four winds, from one end of the sky to the other.*

Fruchtenbaum is correct to be sure, but like DeMar, the implications of his admission are destructive to his futurism. In Isaiah, "the day" that the great trumpet is blown is "the day" in which the Lord *"comes out of his place"* to punish the inhabitants of the earth (the land) for their iniquity. [2] In fact, this is the same resurrection mentioned in the previous chapter (Isaiah 25:8-9), which Paul directly quoted in 1 Corinthians 15:54. Thus, "in the day" when the Lord would

---

1. Arnold Fruchtenbaum, *Israelology: The Missing Link In Systematic Theology*, (Tustin, Calf.; Ariel Ministries Press, 1992), 798-99.
2. Again, my appreciation to Don K. Preston for his great work on the little apocalypse (Isaiah 24-29) in many of his books as it concerns Israel and eschatology.

swallow up death for all time, the great trumpet would be blown. This is exactly what Paul said in 1 Corinthians 15.

> 1 Corinthians 15:52,54
> In a moment, in the twinkling of an eye, *at the last trumpet; 3 for the trumpet will sound, and the dead will be raised imperishable, and we will be changed....* But when this perishable will have put on the imperishable, and this mortal will have put on immortality, *then will come about the saying that is written, "Death is swallowed up in victory.*

Isaiah predicted the second coming of the Lord (out of his place) and the resurrection of Israel, *at the sounding of the great trumpet.* But in Matthew 24:31, *the sounding of the great trumpet* (in fulfillment of Isaiah 27:13) and the gathering together of the elect (a reference to the resurrection) takes place at the fall of Jerusalem in Jesus' generation (24:2-3,34). This means that that second coming of Christ and the resurrection of Israel took place at the sounding of *the great trumpet* in Jesus' generation. But remember, Matthew 24:31 is parallel to Matthew 16:27-28!

Therefore, the coming of the Son of Man in the glory of his Father with his angels to repay every man according to his deeds, took place *at the sounding of the great trumpet* and the resurrection of Israel in Jesus' generation. All these elements found fulfillment at the fall of Jerusalem in AD70 (Luke 21:20-22). The *time* that the great trumpet sounded, was the *time* when the great King descended.

---

3. The *last trumpet* in 1 Corinthians 15 is the *trumpet of God* in 1 Thessalonians 4, which is the *seventh trumpet* in Revelation 11 which is the *great trumpet* in Matthew 24. All four texts place the time of the resurrection at the sounding of a trumpet and the second coming of Christ, in the context of a first century fulfillment.

MATTHEW 16:27-28 = MATTHEW 13
THE WHEAT & THE TARES

Although Matthew 16:27-28 does not serve as a prophetic source for this New Testament prophecy, it would be a great disservice to not at least mention it. Much like the parable of the ten virgins, the wheat and the tares should be understood as a living parable. Jesus, the Son of Man, was at that time through the preaching of the *gospel of the kingdom* planting good seed (the faithful) into his kingdom, the "world" 1 of New Covenant. Based on their response to the kingdom message, the people would later be identified as either wheat or tare. At the end of the Old Covenant age of Judaism in AD70, Israel would be judged and separated, the wicked from the righteous, the wheat from the tares.

The following chart demonstrates that the separation of the wheat from the tares in Matthew 13 is equivalent to the separation of the sheep from the goats in Matthew 25. Regardless of the imagery employed, Jesus was communicating one primary truth; judgment was coming upon Israel in their generation.

MATTHEW 24-25	MATTHEW 13:37-43
Coming of the Son of Man (24:30, 25:31)	Coming of the Son of Man (13:40-41) (Matthew 24:3,30-31 - parallel passage)
Will send forth his angels (24:31)	Will send forth his angels (13:31)
Judgment of sheep and goats (25:32-33)	Judgment of wheat and tares (13:30)
Judgment of all nations (25:32)	Judgment of the "world" (13:38)
Gather together the elect (24:30)	Gather the wheat into the barn (13:30)
Goats sent to eternal fire (25:41)	Tares are burned with fire (13:30)
Sheep inherit the kingdom (25:34)	Righteous shine in the kingdom (13:43)
Fulfilled at the end of the age, in Jesus' generation (24:3,6,14)	Fulfilled at the end of the age (13:39-40)

1. In verse 38 of Matthew 13, the Greek word translated as "world" is "kosmos", and means "a harmonious arrangement or constitution, order, an adornment". Thus, the preaching of the *gospel of the kingdom* was producing "sons of the kingdom" (wheat) within the constitution (world) of the New Covenant-kingdom. The "tares" represent the good seed turned apostate. Although they grew together in the kingdom alongside the wheat, they would be plucked up and cast out at the end-of-the-age-harvest of Israel, in AD70. Paul reiterates this parable in Galatians 4. The tares, (Old Covenant Israel) who had masqueraded as wheat for decades were about to be cast out of the kingdom, while the *true wheat* (the righteous remnant of Israel) was gathered into the barn.

Obviously, the separation of the wheat from the tares in Matthew 13, is in fact the separation of the sheep from the goats in Matthew 25 and takes place at the end of the Jewish age in AD70. But, the separation of the sheep from the goats in Matthew 25 is the judgment of "every man according to their works" in Matthew 16:27-28. This means that the coming of the Son of Man in Matthew 16:27-28 was fulfilled at judgment and separation of Israel at the end of the Jewish age in AD70. The next chart establishes the perfect harmony within all three passages.

MATTHEW 24-25	MATTHEW 13:37-43	MATTHEW 16:27-28
Coming of the Son of Man (24:30, 25:31)	Coming of the Son of Man (implied in the text)	Coming of the Son of Man (16:27-28
Judgment of all nations, Sheep and goats (25:31-33)	Judgment of wheat and tares (13:30,40-43)	Judgment of all men (16:27)
With the angels (24:31, 25:31)	With the angels (13:39-42)	With the angels (16:27)
To establish the kingdom (25:34)	To establish the kingdom (13:41-43)	To establish the kingdom (16:28)
Fulfilled in Jesus' generation at the fall of Jerusalem and the end of the age (24:3,34)	Fulfilled at the end of the age (the harvest) (13:39-40)	Fulfilled in the lifetime of Jesus' first century disciples (16:28)

In Matthew 13 the *coming* of the Son of Man (implied in the text), the sending forth of his angels, and the judgment of the wheat and the tares takes place at the "end of the age". 2 In the Olivet discourse, Jesus placed his *coming*, the sending forth of his angels and the judgment of the sheep and the goats at the "end of the age", in his generation. The same is true in Matthew 16. The *coming* of the Son of Man with his angels to repay every man according to his deeds (the judgment of all nations) takes place in the lifetime of Jesus' contemporary disciples.

---

2. The Greek word translated "end" is "synteleia" and according to Thayer's Lexicon means, "completion, consummation, end". Jesus, who appeared at the "end" (synteleia) of the Jewish age" (Galatians 4:4, Hebrews 9:26) placed its prophetic consummation (synteleia) in his generation (Matthew 24:3,6,13-14,33-34). The end of the Jewish age would result in the second coming of Christ and the resurrection of Israel out from among the dead. Said another way, the second coming of Christ would bring to fulfillment the hope of the Jewish age.

119

Once again, we have undeniable biblical proof that the second coming of Christ in Matthew 25:31 in fulfillment of Matthew 16:27-28 and Matthew 13, was fulfilled at the consummation of the Old Covenant age in AD70. And as we'll see next, this end of the age judgment was Israel's end of the age *harvest*.

A CLOSER LOOK AT MATTHEW 13
THE HARVEST & THE END OF THE AGE

Matthew 13:30,39
Allow both to grow together until the harvest; and in the time of the harvest
I will say to the reapers, "First gather up the tares and bind them in
bundles to burn them up; but gather the wheat into my barn... *the*
harvest is the end of the age..."

According to Jesus in Matthew 13, the judgment takes place at the time of the
harvest; and the harvest is "the end of the age". And, since the end of the age
was the end of the *Jewish age* in AD70, then the harvest must have been reaped
(gathered) in AD70. This being true, what we should expect to find in the pages
of the New Testament is *the expectation of a first century harvest*. Not surprisingly,
this is precisely what we find. And by the way, since the harvest is synchronous
with "the coming" (Matthew 24:30-31, 25:31-33), then to identify the *time* of the
harvest is to identify the *time* of His coming.

In John 4, the city of Sychar in the region of Samaria receives the gospel of the
kingdom.1 In this context, Jesus told his disciples that the time for the harvest had
come; others had labored, yet it was they themselves who would reap the harvest.
Others had sown, but it was they who would *enter into*2 their labor. In Matthew
9-10 Jesus unambiguously drew from Numbers 27 3 when he appointed and
empowered his twelve apostles to assist in his end of the age harvest. Jesus
envisioned a first century harvest to be reaped at the end of the second exodus.

---

1. John 4:5,39-42
2. To *"enter into* their labor" refers not only to the disciples continuing where
   others (the prophets) had left off; but to *their own entrance into* that harvest.
   Through the harvest, they themselves were *entering into* what others before them
   had labored for - the kingdom of God, the restoration of Israel. The ingathering
   of the end of the age harvest would bring about the reaping of their own
   salvation.
3. The parallels between Matthew 9:36-10:7 and Numbers 27:15-23 within the
   context of exodus, kingdom and harvest are amazing. Jesus as the second- Moses
   was appointing men (12 apostles) over the congregation of the new- Israel to
   lead them into their true inheritance through a second exodus. The harvest in
   Matthew 9-10 as well as Matthew 13, was the gathering of the elect of Israel
   out of Egypt (Old Covenant Jerusalem) and into the New Covenant kingdom at
   the end of the Jewish age through the second exodus. When the exodus was
   accomplished, the harvest was reaped. (See the parallel chart on these two texts
   on my website, www.reformedeschatology.com).

The fact that this harvest concerned the gathering of Jews out of Judaism and into the kingdom of God is evident in these words of Jesus....

> Matthew 9:37-38, 10:5-7
> "Then he said to his disciples, *the harvest is plentiful, but the workers are few. Therefore, beseech the Lord of the harvest to send out workers into his harvest....* Do not go in the way of the Gentiles, and do not enter any city of the Samaritans; *but rather go to the lost sheep of the house of Israel. And as you go, preach, saying, 'The kingdom of heaven is at hand.'*"

In Revelation 14 John places the harvest at the hour of God's judgment of Babylon (Old Covenant Israel), the rewarding of the saints (their entering into rest 4), and the cloud-coming of the Son of Man. As we have demonstrated above, all three of these elements find fulfillment at the end of the Jewish age in AD70. Furthermore, the fact that Jesus connects the end of the age harvest in Matthew 13 with Daniel's "time of the end", is highly significant. This means that the righteous inherit the kingdom (shine forth... in the kingdom) in fulfillment of Daniel 12, at the time of the harvest. Put another way, Daniel 12 predicts the harvest which finds fulfillment at the end of the Jewish age in AD70. Notice the parallels....

> "Then *the righteous will shine forth as the son in the kingdom* of their Father. He who has ears, let him hear." (Matthew 13:43)

> *Those who have insight will shine brightly like the brightness of the expanse of heaven,* and those who lead the many to righteousness, *like the stars forever and ever.* (Daniel 12:3)

According to Daniel, those who had insight (those written in the book) would shine brightly in the kingdom5 when the power of Israel (Daniel's holy people)

---

4. Revelation 14:6-20. The mention of "rest" for those who die in the Lord from now on in Revelation 14:13 is a direct echo of Daniel 12:13. Daniel was told that at the "time of the end" he would "rise into *rest*" and receive his "allotted portion" (his inheritance). Daniel was told that this would be accomplished when the power of Israel was completely shattered. Israel's covenant authority was broken in AD70, at the end of the Jewish age.
5. Although "kingdom" is not explicitly stated in the text, it is nonetheless implied. The elements of resurrection and reward (12:2,13) are indicative that the passage concerns the full establishment of the kingdom.

had been completely shattered. The question is, what was their "power,"6 and how and when would that power shattered? I suggest that the "power" of Israel was their covenant union with Yahweh which invested the nation with authority from heaven. That power was forever shattered in AD70, through the removal of the Old Covenant world of Judaism. 7 This means that the righteous inherited the kingdom, in fulfillment of Daniel 12, at the fall of Jerusalem in AD70.

This also agrees perfectly with the parable of the Lord in Matthew 13. Jesus quoting Daniel, said that the righteous would inherit the kingdom at the time of harvest, which was the end of the Jewish age. Therefore, the end of the age harvest of Matthew 13 was fulfilled in AD70, when the covenant-power of the Jews (the tares) was shattered, and the righteous (the wheat) inherited the kingdom. Before we move on, let's briefly consider what the Baptizer had to say concerning Israel's last day's harvest. John said of Jesus....

> Matthew 3:10,12
> The axe is already laid at the root of the trees; therefore, every tree that does not bear good fruit is cut down and thrown into the fire. His winnowing fork is in His hand, and He will thoroughly clear His threshing floor; and *He will gather His wheat into the barn, but He will burn up the chaff with unquenchable fire."*

---

6. The Hebrew word for power is "yad" and means, "hand" (strength or power by implication). The Hebrew word for shattering is "naphats" and means, "to break in pieces, scatter, shatter, disperse". Therefore, we can understand this "shattering of power" as a "breaking apart of hands". Through covenant, Israel had walked "hand in hand" and "face to face" in fellowship with Yahweh. The dissolution of that covenant would mean *a break in "right hand of fellowship"*, and a loss of covenant-authority.

7. In the context of Daniel 12, the shattering of Israel's power must be understood as the result of Israel's time of distress (12:1). Thus, Israel's power (covenant authority) would be completely broken when the "time of distress such as never occurred since there was a nation until that time" was finished. In Matthew 24:21 Jesus quoted Daniel 12:1 verbatim and identified that time of distress as the great tribulation. And, in Luke 21:20-24, Jesus identified the great tribulation as the 1st century siege of Jerusalem which historically lasted three and a half years culminating in AD70. Therefore, Israel's covenant power was forever broken in AD70. There is perfect correlation between Daniel's time of distress which would last for "time, times and a half a time" (three and a half years) at the time of the end, and Jesus' great tribulation which historically lasted for three and a half years during the Roman-Jewish war between 76- 70AD, at the end of the age. This proves that Daniel's "time of the end" was *the time of Israel's end*, and the end of the Old Covenant age of Judaism.

According to John, Jesus himself would accomplish the harvest-separation of Israel through the "wrath" that was about to come, which did come, approximately forty years later. 8 This happened in fulfillment of the word of Malachi, who predicted the appearance of Elijah the prophet before the second coming of Christ to execute the great and terrible day of the Lord. 9

> Malachi 4:1,5
> For behold, *the day is coming, burning like a furnace; and all the arrogant and every evildoer will be chaff;* and the day that is coming will set them ablaze, says the Lord of hosts, so that it will leave them neither root nor branch. Behold, I am going to *send you Elijah the prophet before the coming of the great and terrible day of the Lord.*

Now follow me on this. Malachi predicted the coming of Elijah before the harvest of Israel and the day of the Lord. John came as Elijah, 10 and predicted the harvest of Israel through the wrath that was "about to come". Jesus, drawing from both John and Malachi, predicted the harvest of Israel in the day of judgment at the end of the Jewish age in AD70. (Matthew 13) Therefore, the parable of the wheat and tares prophesied the harvest-judgment of Israel at the day of the Lord, that is, at the second coming of Christ, in fulfillment of Malachi 3-4. And according to Jesus, the parable of the wheat and tares was fulfilled at the end of the Jewish age in AD70.

In conclusion, the second coming of Christ as prophesied in Matthew 16:27-28 was accomplished at the end of the age harvest in AD70, in fulfillment of Matthew 13. The judgment of the *wheat and the tares* was the judgment of *every man* according to their deeds. Having established our position from the Apocalypse of John and the prophesies of Jesus, we now turn our investigation to the epistles of the apostle Paul.

---

8. Matthew 3:7. John's words "to come" are a translation of the Greek word "*mello*". Mello carries the idea of imminence: "about to, about to be". John was warning his generation of the wrath of God that did come upon them in their lifetime. See Luke 20:20-24,32 for the coming of the Son of Man (Jesus) in wrath and vengeance upon Israel in AD70.
9. Malachi 3:1-5, 4:5
10. Matthew 11:7-15, 17:10-13 Mark 9:11-13 Luke 1:13-17

MATTHEW 16:27-28 = 1 THESSALONIANS 4:15-17

Permeated throughout the pages of Paul's letters to the Thessalonians, is a theme and framework that we have identified in many, if not all, of the second coming passages we have studied up to this point. Again, that framework is, "persecution-judgment-vindication". As we shall show from both epistles, the coming of the Lord is his coming in judgment to vindicate his suffering saints who had been persecuted for His name's sake, in fulfillment of Matthew 16:27- 28.

Writing from Corinth in approximately AD51, Paul begins by commending the Thessalonians for their "work of faith and labor of love and steadfastness", despite their having "received the word in much tribulation." 1 Like the churches of God in Judea, the church of the Thessalonians had endured the same sufferings by the hands of their own countrymen, that is, from the Jews in Thessalonica. 2 As a result, the wrath of God was about to come upon these Jewish persecutors to the uttermost. 3 In chapter four, the apostle comforts and reassures these disciples concerning their brethren who had fallen asleep, no doubt due in part to persecution, that although they had died prior to the coming of Christ, they would in no way lose their reward. But more than that, Paul reminds them of the promise of Jesus; that although *some would taste death* prior to the Parousia, not all of them would. This assurance given to the Thessalonians was, as Paul put it, "by (according to) the word of the Lord".

---

1. 1 Thessalonians 1:3,6
2. 1 Thessalonians 2:14. The "countrymen" guilty of the sufferings of the Thessalonians are identified as the Jews of Thessalonica in Acts 17. Aa result of Paul's reasoning with the Jews for three Sabbath days, some of them (Jews) were persuaded (in the faith), along with "a large number of the God-fearing Greeks and a number of the leading women" (17:2-4). Consequently, the Jews became jealous, forming a mob they set the city in an uproar and attacked the house of Jason (17:5-8). Thus, the Thessalonians "received the word in much tribulation" which they suffered from the hands of their own countrymen, that is, the Jews of their own city (1 Thessalonians 1:6,2:14).
3. 1 Thessalonians 2:16. The fact that these persecutors of the saints were "filling up the measure of their sins" also clearly identifies them as Jewish persecutors. It was the Jews - those who refused to be gathered - that Jesus said would, "fill up the measure of their father's *guilt*", in his generation (Matthew 23:32-38). Paul affirmed that Jesus' prophecy was being fulfilled through the persecution and suffering of the Thessalonians.

1 Thessalonians 4:15-17

For this we say to you by the word of the Lord, that *we who are alive and remain until the coming of the Lord,* will not precede those who have fallen asleep. For the Lord Himself will descend from heaven with a shout, with *the voice of the archangel and with the trumpet of God,* and the dead in Christ will rise first. Then *we who are alive and remain will be caught up together with them in the clouds.... "*

In my opinion, it was from the following "word of the Lord" that Paul prophesied.

Matthew 24:30-31,34 (NKJV)

Then the sign of the Son of Man will appear in heaven, and then all the tribes of the earth will mourn, and *they will see the Son of Man coming on the clouds of heaven* with power and great glory. And *He will send His angels with a great sound of a trumpet,* 4 and they will gather together His elect from the four winds, from one end of heaven to the other.... Assuredly, I say to you, *this generation will by no means pass away until all these things take place.*

After all, these prophesies are not just similar, they are downright identical. Paul was not preaching a New Covenant hope for the church to be fulfilled at the *end of time*; Paul was preaching the *one* Old Covenant hope of Israel 5 to be fulfilled at the *time of the end*; that is, the end of the Jewish age. Yet amazingly, in another desperate attempt to maintain the doctrine of a yet future bodily return of Jesus, some futurists have denied that these passages prophesy the events.

The following comparative chart stands as a powerful biblical refutation of the

---

4. As mentioned above, Jesus' reference to the "great trumpet" in Matthew 24:31 is a direct quotation to Isaiah 27:13 and the gathering of Israel at the time of harvest (threshing - 27:12). This harvesting of Israel would be at the time of her resurrection (26:19) and her judgment for bloodshed (26:21). Therefore, the coming of the Lord in Matthew 24 takes place at the time of Israel's resurrection and judgment. This is exactly what we find in Paul's Thessalonian epistles. The coming of the Lord takes place at the time of Israel's resurrection (4:13-17) and judgment (5:1-9, 2 Thessalonians 1:3-10). This further proves our point. The Olivet discourse and Paul's letters to the Thessalonians prophesied the same coming of the Lord at the same time to accomplish the same purpose.
5. Acts 28:20, Romans 11:26-27

126

dispensational rapture doctrine,6 that has deceived much of mainstream Christianity in recent years.

1 THESSALONIANS 4:15-17	MATTHEW 24:30-31
The coming (Parousia) of the Lord himself (4:15,17)	The coming (Parousia) of the Son of Man (24:3,30,37,39)
In the clouds (4:17)	On the clouds (24:30)
With the voice of the archangel (4:16)	With the angels (24:31)
With the trumpet of God (4:16)	With a great trumpet (24:31)
To gather those in Christ (4:14,17)	To gather the elect (24:31)
Fulfilled in Paul's generation - some would "remain" until the coming of the Lord (4:15,17)	Fulfilled in the lifetime of Jesus' first century generation (24:34)

Only those looking to advance a futurist agenda would dare to deny the unity of these two prophecies. Undeniably, the coming of the Lord in 1 Thessalonians 4 fulfills the coming of the Son of Man in Matthew 24, especially given the fact that both Jesus and Paul place the fulfillment of their prophecies in the same generation, *their own*. Notice also an important contrast that Paul makes in the Thessalonian text, it is clearly first century audience relevant.

In verses 14 and 15, Paul refers to "those who have fallen asleep", that is, the dead in Christ. But in verses 15 and 17, Paul refers to "we who are alive and remain". Paul is contrasting between the dead and the living; those who had died, and those still alive; *at that time*. Paul's point was, although some of *the Thessalonians* had died (fallen asleep/tasted death) prior to the Parousia, not all of *them* would. When this contrast is honored, it further emphasizes the temporal limitation of the text. The fact that Paul drew from the Olivet Discourse in this Thessalonian letter becomes virtually undeniable when we compare the larger context of both prophecies.

---

6. 1 Thessalonians 4:15-17 is one of the key passages used by the *premillennial Dispensationalists (Zionist)* to support their rapture doctrine. Supposedly, the coming of the Lord in 1 Thessalonians 4 is different in time, nature, and purpose than the coming of the Lord in Matthew 24. The former takes place prior to the great tribulation, is silent/secret, and accomplishes the rapture of the church off the earth. The latter takes place seven years later, is visible and audible, and initiates a one thousand year millennial reign of Jesus from his earthly temple in Jerusalem. The undeniable fact that 1 Thessalonians 4:15- 17 is parallel to both Matthew 16:27-28 and Matthew 24:30-31 completely "shatters the power" of this false Judaizing doctrine.

1 THESSALONIANS 4-5	MATTHEW 24-25
Don't want you to be uninformed (4:13)	See that no one misleads you (24:4)
Coming (Parousia) of the Lord (4:15)	Coming (Parousia) of the Lord (24:30)
Those who have fallen asleep (4:14)	The elect (24:31)
To meet the Lord (4:17)	To meet the bridegroom (25:6)
In the clouds (4:17)	On the clouds (24:30)
With the trumpet of God (4:16)	With a great trumpet (24:31)
Voice of archangel (4:16)	Send forth His angels (24:31)
Caught up together (4:17)	All nations gathered together (25:32)
Dead in Christ raised (4:16)	Sheep placed on right hand (25:33)
For you yourselves know (5:2)	I have told you in advance (24:25)
The day of the Lord (5:2)	The day your Lord is coming (24:42)
Times and seasons (5:1)	Day and hour (24:36)
Then destruction will come (5:3)	Then will be great tribulation (24:21)
A thief in the night (5:2)	A thief in the night (24:43)
Like labor pains (5:3)	The beginning of birth pangs (24:8)
They will not escape (5:3)	Flood took them all away (24:39)
Those who sleep, sleep at night (5:7)	Got drowsy and began to sleep (25:5)
Let us be alert (5:6)	Therefore, be on the alert (24:42)
Those who get drunk (5:7)	Eat and drink with drunkards (24:49)
Sons of light, of the day (5:5)	They took oil with their lamps (25:4)
(Sons) of night, of darkness (5:5)	No oil with their lamps (25:3)
Wicked destined for wrath (5:9)	Wicked to eternal punishment (25:46)
Hope of salvation (5:8)	Saved, inherit kingdom (24:13,25:34)
We who are alive and remain until the coming of the Lord (4:15,17) (Fulfilled in Paul's generation)	This generation will not pass away until all these things take place (24:34) (Fulfilled in Jesus' generation)

Who can deny that what Paul expected was the fulfillment of a *unified (undivided) Olivet discourse* in his generation. Furthermore, Matthew 24-25 was not the only source for Paul's Parousia expectation in his letter to the Thessalonians. As we have seen, Matthew 16:27-28 lies behind many, if not most of the second coming prophesies recorded in the New Testament. This is abundantly true for 1 Thessalonians 4.

Matthew 16:28
Truly I say to you, there are *some of those who are standing here who will not taste death until they see the Son of Man coming in His kingdom.*

1 Thessalonians 4:15
"For this we say to you by the word of the Lord, *that we who are alive and remain until the coming of the Lord...."*

128

It seems more than obvious that Paul's teaching on the Parousia also rested upon this promise of Jesus, that is, upon the word of the Lord. 7 Those of Paul's generation who would remain alive *until* the coming of the Lord, were those of Jesus' generation who would not taste death *until* they saw the coming of the Son of Man. The following comparative chart illustrates that Matthew 16:27-28 served as the prophetic source for *both* the Olivet discourse and 1 Thessalonians 4.

MATTHEW 16	MATTHEW 24	1 THESSALONIANS 4
Coming of the Son of Man (16:27-28)	Coming of the Son of Man (24:30)	Coming of the Lord himself (4:15-16)
With the angels (16:27)	With the angels (24:31)	With the voice of the archangel (4:16)
To repay (reward) with the kingdom (16:27-28)	To gather the elect into the kingdom (24:31, Luke 21:31)	To receive resurrection and salvation (4:16-17. 5:9)
Some standing here will not taste death *until*.... (16:28)	This generation will not pass away *until*.... (24:34)	We who are alive and remain *until*.... (4:15,17)

Despite the traditions of men who seek to nullify the words of Christ, the lips of the righteous bring forth what is acceptable, 8 and the people who know their God will display strength and take action". 9 Therefore, in honor of the truth of God over the traditions of men, I present the following irrefutable argument:

-Matthew 16:27-28 = 1 Thessalonians 4:15-17
-But, 1 Thessalonians 4:15-17 prophesied the second coming of Christ in the lifetime of Pauls' generation.
-*Therefore, Matthew 16:27-28 prophesied the second coming of Christ in the lifetime of Paul's generation, in fulfillment of 1 Thessalonians 4, according to the "word of the Lord".*

---

7. Concerning Paul's phrase "by the word of the Lord" in 1 Thessalonians 4, Guzik says, "Paul emphasized that this was an authoritative command, though we do not know whether Paul received it by direct revelation or if it was *an unrecorded saying of Jesus*. One way or another, this came from Jesus and did not originate with Paul". (emphasis mine). (David Guzik, *Study Guide for 1 Thessalonians 4*, BLB) For Guzik to suggest that Paul's expectation of the coming of Christ in his generation was drawn from an "unrecorded saying of Jesus" is a rather significant oversight to say the least.
8. Daniel 11:32
9. Proverbs 10:32

A CLOSER LOOK AT 1 THESSALONAINS 4
THE RESURRECTION OF 1 CORINTHIANS 15

For those who seek to alleviate the pressure of the previous argument, 1 we submit another passage written by the same apostle into our body of evidence. As already mentioned, Paul preached the one hope of Israel - the hope of the resurrection - promised by God to their fathers. 2 1 Thessalonians 4 not only prophesied the second coming of Christ, but the resurrection of the dead through the destruction of the last enemy, the death of Adam. 3 Below are Paul's parallel passages....

> 1 Thessalonians 4:15-16
> For this we say to you by the word of the Lord, that *we who are alive and remain until the coming of the Lord....* For the Lord Himself will descend from heaven with a shout, with *the voice of the archangel and with the trumpet of God, and the dead in Christ will rise first.*

> 1 Corinthians 15:51-52
> Behold, I tell you a mystery; *we will not all sleep,* but we will all be changed... *for the trumpet will sound, and the dead will be raised imperishable,* and we will be changed.

---

1. Namely the Dispensational Premillennialists (Zionists). I believe that the rapture doctrine is among other things, their desperate attempt to eliminate 1 Thessalonians 4 as a second coming prophecy. After all, if 1 Thessalonians 4 is "rapture" and not Parousia, then neither is Matthew 16:27-28, 24:30-31 etc.; and the imminent time statements of those texts no longer apply to the second coming. However, this false doctrine obviously creates more problems than solutions for the Zionists. For example, the rapture doctrine doesn't eliminate the time statements altogether, it simply applies them to the rapture, thus limiting the rapture to a first century fulfillment rather than the second coming. The Zionists have clearly not thought this through.
2. Ephesians 4:4, Acts 23:6, 24:15, 26:6-8, 28:20.
3. The *death of Adam* was sin death (covenant death) as opposed to biological death (Genesis 2:16-17). Since the death of Adam was the loss of covenant life (spiritual separation from God), then the resurrection in Christ is *the restoration of covenant life* (spiritual restoration to God). This definition of death and resurrection harmonizes perfectly with *the time* (1st century) for the resurrection in both 1 Thessalonians 4 and 1 Corinthians 15.

The coming of the Lord *out of heaven* 4 in 1 Thessalonians 4, is undeniably the second coming of Christ at the time of the resurrection in 1 Corinthians 15. And notice again, both passages *limit* the prophecy to the lifetime of the first century generation.

1 THESSALONIANS 4	1 CORINTHIANS 15
The Parousia of the Lord (4:15)	The Parousia of the Lord (15:23)
The trumpet of God (4:16)	The last trumpet (15:52)
The dead in Christ will rise (4:16)	The dead raised imperishable (15:52)
According to "the word of the Lord" (4:15)	According to the saying "that is written" (15:54)
Some of those who were alive would "remain until" (4:15)	Those who were alive would "not all sleep" (15:51)

Based on these perfect Pauline parallels, consider the following argument:
-The Parousia of the Lord in 1 Thessalonians 4:15-17 = the Parousia of the Lord in 1 Corinthians 15:51-52.

-But, the Parousia of the Lord in 1 Corinthians 15:51-52 refers to the second coming of Christ at the time of the resurrection, in fulfillment of Isaiah 25:8.

-Therefore, the Parousia of the Lord in 1 Thessalonians 4:15-17 refers to the second coming of Christ at the time of the resurrection of 1 Corinthians 15, in fulfillment of Isaiah 25:8.

This being true, consider what follows....
-The Parousia of the Lord in 1 Thessalonians 4:15-17 refers to the second coming of Christ at the time of the resurrection of 1 Corinthians 15.

---

4.   Compare "the Lord himself will descend from heaven" in 1 Thessalonians 4:16, with "the Lord is about to come out from his place" in Isaiah 26:21. As a matter of fact, both 1 Thessalonians 4 and 1 Corinthians 15 can be traced back to Isaiah 62:11. Here are the prophetic progression for both passages: (1) *Isaiah 62:11 - Matthew 24:30-34 - 1 Thessalonians 4.* And, (2) *Isaiah 25:8 - Isaiah 62:11 - 1 Corinthians 15:51-54.* As we have seen, Isaiah 62:11 is also a primary prophetic source for Matthew 16:27-28. This means that coming of the Lord in Matthew 16, 1 Thessalonians 4 and 1 Corinthians 15 all have their biblical roots in Isaiah 62; a prophecy of the second coming of Christ for the salvation and remarriage of Israel.

-But, the Parousia of the Lord in 1 Thessalonians 4:15-17 = the Parousia of the Son of Man in Matthew 24:30-31 and Matthew 16:27-28. 5

-Therefore, both Matthew 16:27-28 and Matthew 24:30-31 prophesied the second coming of Christ at the time of the resurrection of both 1 Corinthians 15 and 1 Thessalonians 4 - in fulfillment of Isaiah 25:8 - and were fulfilled in the lifetime of Jesus' generation (16:28)

The comparative chart on the following page powerfully demonstrates the reality of a first century second coming of Christ in fulfillment of Matthew 16:27-28. The clarity and consistency of this doctrine throughout the New Testament is staggering.

MATTHEW 16	MATTHEW 24	1 THESSALONIANS 4	1 CORINTHIANS 15
Coming of the Son of Man (16:27-28)	Coming of the Son of Man (24:30)	Coming of the Lord himself (4:15-16)	The coming of the Lord (15:23)
With the angels (16:27)	With the angels (24:31)	With the voice of the archangel (4:16)	The last trumpet, the seventh angel (15:52)
The resurrection (repay every man) (16:27)	The resurrection (gather together the elect) (24:31)	The resurrection (dead in Christ rise) (4:16)	The resurrection (dead raised imperishable) (15:52)
Some standing here will not taste death *until they see the Son of Man coming*.... (16:28)	This generation will not pass away *until all these things are fulfilled* (24:34)	We who are alive and remain *until the coming of the Lord* (4:15,17)	We *shall "not all sleep"* but we shall all be changed (15:51)

---

5. Although the Greek word "Parousia" is not used in Matthew 16:27-28, the passage nonetheless prophesies the Parousia event of Christ.

132

MATTHEW 16:27-28 = 2 THESSALONIANS 1:4-10

While still in Corinth in approximately AD52, Paul penned his second letter to the church of the Thessalonians. Evidently their persecution had not abated as Paul once again begins by giving thanks to God and praises the Thessalonians for their "perseverance and faith" amidst severe "persecution and affliction". The apostle then comforts and reassures these suffering saints that God's righteous judgment would prevail at the revelation of Christ, giving them relief from their then present afflictions. Through endurance they would be counted worthy to inherit the kingdom of God. On the other hand, those who were causing their affliction would themselves be repaid with affliction, and in the end, destruction. 1

As in Paul's first letter, the pattern of "persecution-judgment-vindication" is present once again as a dominant theme. The next passage for our investigation is cited below, followed by its obvious prophetic source in the New Testament, Matthew 16:27-28.

> 2 Thessalonians 1:5-8
> "This a plain indication of God's righteous judgment so that you will be considered worthy of the kingdom of God, for which indeed *you are suffering.* For after all it is only just for God *to repay with affliction those who afflict you,* and to give relief to you who are afflicted and to us as well *when the Lord Jesus will be revealed from heaven with His mighty angels in flaming fire...."*

> Matthew 16:27-28
> For *the Son of Man is going* to come in the glory of His Father *with His angels,* and will then repay every man according to his deeds. Truly I say to you, *there are some of those who are standing here who will not taste death until they see the Son of Man coming in His kingdom.*

---

1. 2 Thessalonians 1:5-9. Paul is clearly reiterating the words of Jesus and applying them to the Thessalonian situation. In Luke's account of the Olivet discourse, Jesus warns his disciples of a coming Jewish persecution (21:12), which, if they would endure would lead to life (21:19) through the establishment of the kingdom of God (21:31) at the second coming (21:27). Those who had been their persecutors would at that time suffer the wrath and vengeance of God (21:20-24). Furthermore, to say that God would "repay with affliction those who afflict you" is the same as saying that they would be repaid "according to their deeds" (Matthew 16:27). These are in fact one and the same judgment, as we shall demonstrate below.

At first blush the parallels in these passages may not seem as obvious as some of the others we have seen. However, the comparative chart below brings these seemingly foggy parallels into focus.

MATTHEW 16:27-28	2 THESSALONIANS 1:4-10
Coming of the Son of Man from heaven (16:21,24,27-28)	Revelation of the Lord Jesus from heaven (1:7)
In the glory of his Father (16:27)	In the glory of his power - strength (1:9)
With his angels (16:27)	With his mighty angels (1:7)
To repay every man according to his deeds (16:27)	To repay with affliction and retribution those who afflict you (1:6,8)
To establish and reward the saints with the kingdom (16:28)	To establish and reward the saints with the kingdom (1:5,9-10)
Fulfilled in the lifetime of Jesus' contemporary disciples (16:28)	Fulfilled while the 1st century Thessalonians were still experiencing their 1st century afflictions (1:6-8)

In light if this evidence, consider the following argument which we will fully vindicate below as we take a closer look at the Thessalonian text.

-The revealing of Jesus in 2 Thessalonians 1:4-10 = the coming of the Son of Man in Matthew 16:27-28

-But, the revealing of Jesus in 2 Thessalonians 1:4-10 and prophesied the second coming of Christ in the lifetime of the Thessalonians.

-Therefore, 2 Thessalonians 1:4-10, prophesied the second coming of Christ in fulfillment of Matthew 16:27-28, and placed its fulfillment in the lifetime of the first century Thessalonians, that is, in the lifetime of Jesus' generation.

But even apart from this evidence, 2 Thessalonians 1 is perhaps Paul's most clear-cut prophecy that supports, or should we say, *that proves* a first century second coming of Christ. Consider the following facts at stated in the text:

1. The Thessalonians were *at that present time* enduring suffering through persecutions and afflictions (1:4-7).
2. The Thessalonians would receive relief from those persecutions and afflictions *when the Lord Jesus was revealed from heaven with his mighty angels in flaming fire* (1:7).
3. The Thessalonian persecutors would be repaid with affliction resulting in destruction through the righteous judgment of God, *when the Lord Jesus was revealed from heaven with his might angels in flaming fire.* (1:5-8).

Notice how certain modern translations rightly interpret the present tenses used in this passage....

> This is evidence of the righteous judgment of God, that you may be made worthy of the kingdom of God, for which *you are suffering* (1:5 RSV)

> Since it is a righteous thing with God to give back to *those troubling you* – trouble. (1:6 YLT)

> And God will provide rest for *you who are being persecuted* and also for us when the Lord Jesus appears from heaven.... (1:7 NLT)

> And to *you who are being afflicted* to give rest together with us when the Lord Jesus is revealed from heaven.... (1:7 NET)

Although many pages and could be written concerning this passage,2 I will keep my comments quite brief. The fact is this; while exercising apostolic authority, and while under apostolic inspiration, Paul clearly told the first century Thessalonians that *they themselves* would experience *relief* from their then- present afflictions; and that their then-present persecutors would be *repaid with affliction.... when the Lord Jesus was revealed*3 *from heaven*...! Therefore, if the first century Thessalonians did not *receive relief* from their then-present sufferings at the second coming of Christ *in their lifetime*, then Paul was wrong, Jesus failed, and they should both be condemned as false prophets. The same is true concerning their persecutors. If the Thessalonians' then-present persecutors were not *repaid with affliction* at the second coming of Christ *in their lifetime*, then both Paul and Jesus received exactly what they deserved; martyrdom as false prophets.

---

2. I highly recommend Don K. Preston's book, *"In Flaming Fire"* (Jadon Management Inc., 2005,2011,2015), for an in depth and scholarly exegesis of 2 Thessalonians 1. Be sure to pay special attention to his comments on "thlipsis" (afflictions) and "anesis" (relief) as used in the text. It is a fantastic study.
3. This "revealing" of Jesus in 1:7 is without doubt his second coming, as it occurs "with his angels, in flaming fire". This is also supported by the larger context. In 2:1-2, Paul refers to this "revealing" as the "coming" (Parousia) of the Lord Jesus Christ to "gather together" the Thessalonians (the elect) at the day of the Lord. In Matthew 24:30-34, Jesus places the "gathering together of the elect" (the Thessalonians Christians included) at his coming (Parousia) with his angels, in the lifetime of his contemporary generation.

There is only one conclusion which honors context and vindicates inspiration: The second coming of Christ in Matthew 16:27-28 was accomplished in the lifetime of the first century Thessalonians, bringing both relief (vindication) and retribution (judgment) into that first century situation, in fulfillment of 2 Thessalonians 1.

A CLOSER LOOK AT 2 THESSALONIANS 1
ZEPHANIAH & THE DAY OF THE LORD

2 Thessalonians 1:7
".... when the Lord Jesus will be revealed from heaven with His mighty angels *in flaming fire...."*

For many 21st century Christians in the west, the words "in flaming fire" when used in the context of the coming of the Lord, conjure up the idea of an end of time global meltdown when the entire cosmos goes up in smoke. But this would hardly have been the case for someone living approximately 2000 years ago in the east, especially if they had been subjected to ancient Hebrew thinking, and literature.

In 2 Thessalonians 1, the apostle Paul employed common Old Testament prophetic language to communicate the imminent judgment of Judah and Jerusalem in the day of the Lord. 1 The coming of the Lord *in flaming fire* was well known Hebrew metaphor of the day 2 which Paul's audience would have been familiar with. A great example of this language which is used in the same context is found in the book of Zephaniah. In chapter 1, the prophet predicted the coming of the Lord to *judge Israel by fire,* in the day of the Lord. Notice the specific language in the following passage....

> Zephaniah 1:4,7,12,18
> "So, I will stretch out My hand *against Judah and against all the inhabitants of Jerusalem....* Be silent before the Lord God! *For the day of the Lord is near....* It will come about at that time that *I will search Jerusalem with lamps, and I will punish the men who are stagnant in spirit,* who say in their hearts, the Lord will not do good or evil!' Neither their silver nor their gold will be able to deliver them on the day of the Lord's wrath; and *all the earth will be devoured in the fire of His jealousy...."*

---

1. The coming of the Lord *in flaming fire* in 2 Thessalonians 1 is sandwiched between two passages which mention the "day of the Lord" (1 Thessalonians 5:1-10 - *2 Thessalonians 1:4-10* - 2 Thessalonians 2:1-8). Although not mentioned in the passage itself, it is in *the day of the Lord* that the Lord would come *in flaming fire.*
2. For example, Daniel 7:9-14 Isaiah 30:27-20 Isaiah 66:15-16 and Micah 1:2-7 all use *fire* as a metaphor for his *presence though judgment,* specifically the judgment of Yahweh against Israel.

Zephaniah predicted the judgment of *Judah and Jerusalem*. Zephaniah predicted the coming of the Lord 3 *in fire*, in the day of the Lord. Zephaniah placed the fulfillment of his prophecy *near* in his day. Zephaniah's prophecy found fulfillment when Jerusalem, both city and temple, was destroyed by the Babylonians in 586BC, in Zephaniah's generation. Now ask yourself the following questions:

Did the fulfillment of this day of the Lord in Zephaniah require Yahweh to come literally and bodily out of heaven to search out Jerusalem for scoundrels? Clearly not. Was "all the earth" literally devoured by fire, and did "all the inhabitants of the earth" literally come to a "complete end" when this prophecy was fulfilled in the 6th century BC? Or course not. This means that Zephaniah's prophecy was not fulfilled literally, but metaphorically. 4 Through the fiery destruction of Jerusalem by Babylon, the Lord's *covenant-presence* was revealed, that is, the Lord came against Jerusalem in covenant-judgment. This historical event *revealed the Lord in fire*, and Zephaniah called it the day of the Lord. I suggest this is precisely how Paul's words must be understood in 2 Thessalonians 1.

Like Zephaniah, Paul predicted the judgment of *the Jews* (the persecutors of the church). Like Zephaniah, Paul predicted the coming of the Lord *in fire*, in the day of the Lord. And like Zephaniah, Paul placed the fulfillment of his prophecy *near* in his day; that is, in the lifetime of the Thessalonians of Paul's generation. Now ask yourself this question. If both Zephaniah and Paul used the exact same language in the exact same context limited to the exact same time (their generation), then why could Zephaniah's prophecy be fulfilled *metaphorically in-time*, while Paul's prophecy *must* be fulfilled *literally at the end of time*? While you ponder the question, consider the genuine parallels on the following chart found within the larger contexts of these prophesies.

---

3. Although not mentioned explicitly, Zephaniah 1 alludes to the coming of the Lord. In verse 12f, the Lord says that he would *"search Jerusalem with lamps"* to punish those who have sinned against him. The imagery of the text pictures the Lord as being *present* among his people in a time of *visitation* and *inspection*. (Compare Genesis 18:17-32, Luke 19:41-44 and 1 Peter 2:12). Besides this, in chapter 3 Zephaniah plainly says that through this judgment the Lord would be *in their midst* as a "victorious warrior" (3:8-12).
4. Once again, see Don K. Preston's book, *"In Flaming Fire"*, where he more fully develops the nature of the day of the Lord in both Old and New Testaments, in the context of the coming of the Lord.

2 THESSALONIANS 1-2	ZEPHANIAH 1-3
The day of the Lord (2:2)	The day of the Lord (1:7,14)
The coming (revealing) of the Lord (1:7)	The Lord "searches" Jerusalem, the Lord is in your midst (1:12, 3:15-17)
Retribution and destruction in flaming fire (1:7-9)	Inhabitants of the earth (land) devoured in the fire of his zeal and indignation (1:18, 3:8)
To repay the persecutors with affliction and destruction (1:6,9)	To punish and bring distress on those who fill the house of the Lord with violence (1:9,17)
To bring relief and glory to the faithful -the remnant- (1:7,10)	To restore the fortunes of the remnant -the faithful- (2:7)
To be fulfilled in the lifetime of the Thessalonians, while *they* were still suffering persecution (1:4-8)	Fulfilled "very quickly", in the lifetime of some who heard the prophecy - 586BC (1:14)

Paul was a prophet who employed the common prophetic language of his day to communicate to the people of his day that Yahweh's judgment was about to be poured out upon Judah and Jerusalem in the day of the Lord. Like Zephaniah, Paul's prophecy found historical fulfillment in his generation when Jerusalem was plowed like a field, 5 and the temple was burned *with fire* by the Romans in AD70. Through that fiery judgment, *the covenant-presence of Christ* was revealed from heaven in flaming fire, bringing relief to the saints and affliction to their persecutors.

Therefore, the revealing of Christ with his angels in flaming fire in 2 Thessalonians 1, does not demand the bodily reappearing of Jesus the son of Joseph sometime in our future. As a matter of fact, Paul's usage of metaphoric language taken from Zephaniah's prophecy, coupled with the imminent historical judgment of Jerusalem in the first century, demands just the opposite. The Lord's *presence* was once again about to be *revealed in fire* through the covenant-judgment of Jerusalem and the vindication of the remnant. For those who had eyes to see, the Lord Jesus *was* revealed from heaven with his mighty angels *in flaming fire* during the Jewish-Roman war between 67-70AD.

In conclusion, using highly metaphoric yet commonplace language of their day, both Zephaniah and Paul prophesied an in-time (not end of time) day of the

---

5.   Jeremiah 26:18, Micah 3:12

Lord 6 that came to pass in the lifetime of their contemporary generations. Therefore, since Matthew 16:27-28 served as prophetic source for 2 Thessalonians 1, and since 2 Thessalonians 1 prophesied the second coming of Christ in AD70, then Matthew 16:27-28 prophesied the second coming of Christ and was fulfilled in AD70.

---

6. This is not only true for *the day of the Lord* in Thessalonians, it is true for every *day of the Lord prophecy* in the New Testament. The *nature* in which the "day of the Lord prophesies" were fulfilled in the Old Testament, provides the proper hermeneutic to interpret *the nature of fulfillment* for the *"day of the Lord prophecies"* in the New.

ISAIAH & FLAMES OF FIRE

Like Zephaniah, Isaiah also prophesied the coming of the Lord *in flaming fire* to bring judgment upon his enemies and comfort to his servants. As we shall see, Paul's language in 2 Thessalonians 1 was taken directly from this Old Testament prophet, and is another great example of ancient apocalyptic metaphor in the New Testament. Below are the parallel prophesies.

Isaiah 66:6,15-16
A voice of uproar from the city, a voice from the temple, the voice of the Lord who is rendering recompense to His enemies.... For behold, *the Lord will come in fire* and His chariots like the whirlwind, *to render His anger with fury, and His rebuke with flames of fire.* For the Lord will *execute judgment by fire* and by His sword on all flesh, and those slain by the Lord will be many.

2 Thessalonians 1:6-8
For after all it is just for God *to repay with affliction those who afflict you,* and to give relief to you who are afflicted and to us as well *when the Lord Jesus will be revealed from heaven with His mighty angels in flaming fire, dealing out retribution to those who do not know God and to those who do not obey the gospel of our Lord Jesus.*

Paul made sure that his contemporary Thessalonians understood *the connection* between Isaiah's prophecy and what they were expecting to occur within their own lifetime. The comparative chart below confirms that the apostle Paul most assuredly had Isaiah's prophecy in mind when he wrote to comfort and encourage these persecuted yet faithful believers.

2 THESSALONIANS 1:4-8	ISAIAH 66:6-16
The coming (revealing) of the Lord in flaming fire (1:7)	The coming of the Lord in flaming fire (66:15)
To repay with affliction those who afflict you (1:6)	To render recompense to his enemies (66:6)
Eternal destruction (1:9)	Their worm will not die, fire will not be quenched (66:24)
Relief to his afflicted servants (1:7)	Comfort to his servants (66:13)
The glory and power of the Lord revealed (1:9-10)	The glory and power of the Lord revealed (66:14,18)
Fulfilled in the lifetime of the Thessalonians, while *they* were suffering their then-present persecution (1:4-8)	Fulfilled when the Lord's enemies were slain and His servants called by another name (65:16, 66:14-16)

Unlike Zephaniah, who predicted an imminent (in his generation) judgment of Judah and Jerusalem, Isaiah predicted the *eschatological* (last days) judgment and destruction of both city and nation to establish the new creation, the new heavens and the new earth. 1 In other words, Isaiah 66 prophesied the second coming of Christ. 2 However, since 2 Thessalonians 1 drew from Isaiah 66, and since Matthew 16:27-28 served as a source for 2 Thessalonians 1, then both 2 Thessalonians 1 and Matthew 16:27-28 predicted the second coming of Christ in fulfillment of Isaiah 66. To confirm this conclusion, we will look at the evidence within the larger context of Isaiah's prophecy, specifically, when the Lord would come.... with "flames of fire".

> Isaiah 65:14-15,17 66:15
> Behold, my servants will shout joyfully with a glad heart, but you will cry out with a heavy heart, and you will wail with a broken spirit. *You will leave your name for a curse to My chosen ones, and the Lord God will slay you.* But My servants will be called by another name. For behold, *I create new heavens and a new earth; and the former things will not be remembered or come to mind....* For behold, *the Lord will come in fire and His chariots like the whirlwind, to render His anger with fury, and His rebuke with flames of fire.*

According to Isaiah there would be a final and decisive separation between the rebellious and the faithful of Israel at the coming of the Lord. Those who had become the enemies of the Lord would forfeit their name (their identity), while His servants (the righteous remnant) would be called (known) by another name (a new identity). Said another way, *there would be a transfer and transformation of identity among the people of God.* 3

---

1. The coming of the Lord in flaming fire in judgment of his enemies in Isaiah 66, is the judgment and destruction of the rebellious of Israel resulting in the establishment of the new creation in Isaiah 65:1-19. These chapters (and more) form a united prophecy.
2. Commentators are unanimously agreed that Isaiah 65-66 serves as Peter's primary source for his prophecy of the new heavens and new earth at the second coming (Parousia) of Christ in 2 Peter 3.
3. The theme of "identity transfer and transformation" runs through the entirety of the Bible and specifically the New Testament. For example, *the true Israel* were identified as those who followed Jesus, the prophet like Moses (Acts 3:22-26), as those who were born according to the promise by faith (Romans 9:6-9) as opposed to the flesh by law, and as those who had been circumcised in heart, inwardly, rather than outwardly (Romans 2:29). Those whose received this identity transfer, received an identity transformation (2 Corinthians 3:18, Romans 8:29, 1 Corinthians 15:49-54) at the second coming of Christ.

For the astute reader, the connection between this prophecy of Isaiah and the parables of Jesus, specifically those in Matthew 21 and 22, can hardly be missed. The following chart demonstrates that Jesus predicted the fulfillment of the coming of the Lord in Isaiah 65-66, and placed its fulfillment at the *"slaying"* of enemies who pierced him.

ISAIAH 65-66	MATTHEW 21-22
Spread out His hands all day long, called but no one answered (65:2)	He sent out his slaves, he sent other slaves, they paid no attention (21:34-37, 22:2-6)
The coming of the Lord (66:15)	The coming of the Lord (21:40, 22:11)
To execute judgment by fire (66:16)	To set their city on fire (22:7)
Will render recompense to his enemies, will slay many (65:15, 66:6,16)	Will bring those wretches to a wretched end, destroyed those murderers (21:41, 22:7)
The name (identity) of the Jews would be removed (vacated/relinquished) (65:15)	Kingdom taken from Israel, the unprepared removed from the wedding (21:43, 22:11-13)
The Lord's servants called by another name (given a new identity) (65:15)	Wedding takes place - those clothed in Christ are given a new identity (22:10-12)
New heaven and earth established (65:17-19)	Kingdom established and inherited (21:43)
	Fulfilled when those who had killed Jesus were destroyed and their city burned (22:7) - AD70

In these two parables, Jesus predicted a *transfer and transformation of identity* 4 for the sons of the kingdom at his coming in fiery-judgment 5 in fulfillment of Isaiah. In Matthew 21 the emphasis is *identity transfer*; the kingdom is given to the saints and they are at that time *revealed* (identified) as sons of God. In Matthew 22 the emphasis is *identity transformation*; the marriage takes place when the saints are clothed for the wedding, and are at that time *conformed (transformed)*

---

4. Their *identity transformation* took place on a purely spiritual level, when the mortal put on immortality, while their *identity transfer* took place on a more practical level; as their *revealing* as sons of God to the nations.
5. In Isaiah, it is the Lord who executes *judgment by fire*. In Matthew, the Lord executes *judgment by fire* by sending his armies to burn the city. In other words, the Lord comes in fire through the fiery-judgment of his armies.

into sons of God, 6 in the image of Christ. 7 And notice, the fulfillment of these parables is placed at the fall of Jerusalem in AD70, when those who had killed him were judged, and their city burned with fire. This means that Isaiah 65-66, the source for Jesus' parables, must have been fulfilled by that time also. The *time* when Jerusalem was *burned with fire,* identifies the *time* when the Lord *came in fire.*

With this established, consider the following arguments:
-The coming of the Lord in Matthew 21-22 = the second coming of the Lord in flaming fire to establish the new creation in Isaiah 65-66.

-But, the coming of the Lord in the parables of Jesus were fulfilled in AD70, when those who killed Jesus were judged, and their city burned with fire.

-Therefore, the second coming of the Lord in flaming fire to establish the new creation in Isaiah 65-66 was fulfilled in AD70, when those who killed Jesus were judged, and Jerusalem burned with fire.

Based on this conclusion, consider the next argument:
- The second coming of the Lord in flaming fire to establish the new creation in Isaiah 65-66 was fulfilled in AD70, when those who killed Jesus were judged, and Jerusalem burned with fire.

-But, the second coming of the Lord in flaming fire to establish the new creation in Isaiah 65-66 = the revealing of Christ in flaming fire in 2 Thessalonians 1.

-Therefore, the revealing of Christ in flaming fire in 2 Thessalonians 1 was the second coming of the Lord to establish the new creation in fulfillment of Isaiah 65-66, and was fulfilled in AD70; when those who killed Jesus were judged and their city was burned with fire.

In conclusion: The coming of the Lord in flaming fire in Isaiah 65-66 predicted the second coming of Christ in AD70. Therefore, since 2 Thessalonians 1 drew from Isaiah 66, and since Matthew 16:27-28 served as a source for 2 Thessalonians 1, then both 2 Thessalonians 1 and Matthew 16:27-28 predicted the second coming of Christ in flaming fire to bring in the new creation. The new heavens and new earth arrived in the lifetime of Jesus' generation. 8

---

6. Romans 8:29.
7. 2 Corinthians 3:18, Romans 8:29, 1 Corinthians 15:49
8. Hebrews 12:22-28, Revelation 21:1-3, 22:6-12

MATTHEW 16:27-28 = 2 TIMOTHY 4:1

2 Timothy was perhaps the last letter written by the apostle Paul prior to his martyrdom under emperor Nero. Thus, it is fitting that 2 Timothy 4:1 should be the final passage we study in our investigation of the doctrine of the second coming of Christ. We will now attempt to demonstrate, that Paul, in anticipation of a first century Parousia, drew directly from the words of Jesus in Matthew 16:27-28. Notice again the similarities between the words of Jesus and the words of Paul.

> Matthew 16:27-28
> *For the Son of Man is going to come* in the glory of His Father with His angels, and will then *repay every man according to His deeds.* Truly I say to you, there are some of those who are standing here who will not taste death until they see *the Son of Man coming in His kingdom.*

> 2 Timothy 4:1
> I solemnly charge you in the presence of God and of Christ Jesus, *who is to judge the living and the dead, and by His appearing and his kingdom.*

This is another example of where the parallels are not so "in-your-face-obvious". However, by comparing themes rather than just words, as has been our approach through this book, the parallels become more than evident. Notice the following chart....

MATTHEW 16:27-28	2 TIMOTHY 4:1
The coming of the Son of Man	The appearing of Jesus
To judge the living and dead (to repay every man)	*About to* judge the living and the dead (resurrection)
To establish the kingdom	To establish the kingdom
Christ was *"about to come"* (from the Greek word "mello") in that generation	*"About to be"* fulfilled in 1st century (from the Greek word "mello")

Both Matthew 16:27-28 and 2 Timothy 4:1 contain the "big three" eschatological themes/events; which are:

1. The second coming (revelation)
2. The judgment and resurrection (retribution)
3. The establishment of the kingdom (reward)

But notice what this means....
-Matthew 16:27-28 = 2 Timothy 4:1

-But, 2 Timothy 4:1 prophesied the fulfillment of the "big three" of eschatology, the second coming, the kingdom, the judgment and resurrection.

-Therefore, Matthew 16:27-28 prophesied the second coming of Christ to establish the kingdom at the judgment and resurrection, and placed its fulfillment in the lifetime of Jesus' generation.

Interestingly, both Jesus and Paul used the same Greek verb (*mello*) to express the imminence of their prophesies. In the NASB the word *mello* is translated, "*is to*" in both passages. However, "*is to*" is a poor translation of this word and does not capture the full force of what Paul was communicating. The word *mello* properly means "to be about to, to be on the point of". In other words, *mello* better conveys the idea of imminence rather than certainty. Notice how Young's translates both passages.

> 2 Timothy 4:1 (YLT)
> I do fully testify, then, before God, and the Lord Jesus Christ, who *is about to* judge the living and dead at his manifestation and his reign.

> Matthew 16:27(YLT)
> For, the Son of Man *is about to* come in the glory of his Father, with his messengers, and then he will reward each, according to his work.

Thus, in Matthew 16:27-28, Jesus promised that his coming in glory to establish his kingdom and judge all men, was *about to* occur in the lifetime of his first disciples. Paul, living in that same generation told Timothy that the appearing of Jesus to establish his kingdom and judge all men, the living and the dead, was *about to* take place. Thus, we have perfect harmony between the two texts. 1 Yet there is more. Peter says the same thing in his first epistle. Notice the consistency in both Peter and Paul's message; the parallel passages are cited on the following page.

---

1. This "appearing" of Christ and the judgment "about to" come (2 Timothy 4:1) is his appearing "out of second" (from the most holy place - Hebrews 9:28) to bring both judgment and salvation in a "very little while" (Hebrews 10:37). Thus, we have additional support for Paul's expectation of a first century second coming. Both these passages are simply a reiteration what Jesus had promised in Matthew 16:27-28 to be accomplished in his generation, in fulfillment of Isaiah 59, 62 etc.

2 Timothy 4:1 (DBY)

"I testify before God and Christ Jesus, *who is about to judge the living and dead....*"

1 Peter 4:5

"But they will give account to Him *who is ready to judge the living and the dead.*"

The word that Peter used translated as "ready" is the Greek word "hetoimos" and means exactly what is says, "to be ready, in readiness". 2 Therefore, concerning "the appointed time 3 for the judgment 4 of the living and the dead at the second coming of Christ; Peter said Jesus was "*ready*", Paul said he was "*about to*", and Jesus said some who were standing there would "*not taste death*" until it had come to pass.

Despite this three-fold inspired testimony, we continue to be told dogmatically by all futurist camps that the second coming of Christ is still in our future. Yet, if the infallibility of scripture means anything, this simply cannot be true. We have shown time and again, that every second coming passage which we have paralleled with Matthew 16:27-28 stands valid based on much more than just similarity of language. The parallels within these passages are self-confirmed based on the identical themes and framework found within their larger contexts; specifically, "persecution- judgment-vindication". The same holds true for this passage in 2 Timothy.

Recall the immediate context of Matthew 16:27-28. Jesus foretold his own suffering and the suffering of his disciples at the hands of the leaders in Jerusalem (16:21-26). The Divine response would be the *coming* of Christ in

---

2. Thayer's Greek Lexicon. Significantly, both times (2x) this word is used in the New Testament outside of 1 Peter 4:5, it carries the idea of being *both* morally prepared and temporally ready. The meaning in 1 Peter 4:5 is no different.
3. Gr. "*kairos*" (1 Peter 4:17) means an appointed/set time, as opposed to "*chronos*" meaning time in general.
4. "The judgment" (1 Peter 4:17) is what is known as an "anaphoric reference", the anaphoric article being "judgment" in 1 Peter 4:5. I simply make mention of this technical point, the reader is encouraged to dig into the significance of the anaphoric reference within this context for themselves. Simply stated, "judgment" in Peter in 4:17 points back to "the judgment" of 1 Peter 4:5. This means that the judgment that was ready to be executed in its appointed time was "*the judgment" of the living and the dead.* This agrees perfectly with what Paul says in 2 Timothy 4:1.

judgment of those persecutors (16:27) and in vindication of the saints who had suffered (16:28). It is in this framework that Paul quotes Jesus in 2 Timothy 4:1. Like Jesus, Paul encouraged his young disciple Timothy to join him in his sufferings for the sake of the gospel (1:8,12 2:3). Like Jesus, Paul taught that death to sin and endurance through sufferings would bring salvation and glory (2:10-11). If they endured like Him they would reign with Him, (2:12) and gain entrance into the kingdom (4:18). Like Jesus, Paul identified the second coming event as his coming to bring judgment on their persecutors, but reward and vindication to saints; which Jesus himself placed in Paul's own generation.

As a matter of fact, 2 Timothy 2:11-12 is Paul's inspired paraphrase of Jesus' words in Matthew 16:24-25. Consider the following chart which illustrates the parallel themes of persecution-judgment-vindication, found within the larger contexts of both Matthew 16:27-28 and 2 Timothy 4:1.

2 TIMOTHY 2:11-12	MATTHEW 16:24-25
Those who died with Him would live with Him (2:11) - persecution/suffering	Those who would lose their life would find it (16:25) - persecution/suffering
Those who denied Him, He would likewise deny (2:12) - judgment	Those who would save their life would lose it (16:25) - judgment
Those who would endure would reign with Him (2:12) - vindication	Those who would follow Him would "come after Him" (16:24) - vindication
	Fulfilled in the lifetime of Jesus' first century contemporary generation (16:28)

There is no doubt whatsoever that this imminent judgment of Christ and his appearing in his kingdom, was Paul's prophetic reiteration of the first century second coming of Christ as prophesied by Jesus in Matthew 16:27-28.

A CLOSER LOOK AT 2 TIMOTHY 4
ALEXANDER THE COPPERSMITH

Recall that in Matthew 26:64, Jesus told Caiaphas and the body of the Sanhedrin that they would see him coming on the clouds of heaven in judgment against them. 1 In other words, Jesus taught that *his own persecutors* would be repaid "according to their deeds" in their lifetime, in fulfillment of Matthew 16:27-28. Well, so did Paul; only Paul took Jesus' words one step further. Paul went so far as to *name* one of his own persecutors who was about to be judged *according to his deeds,* in fulfillment of Matthew 16:27-28. This has incredible implications!

In 2 Timothy 4:14, Paul specifically identified *Alexander the coppersmith* 2 as an enemy of the faith and one of his own grievous persecutors.

> "Alexander the coppersmith *did me much harm....*"

But who was this Alexander? Matthew Henry, commenting on the Alexander of Acts 19:33 says, "Some think this Alexander had been a Christian, but had apostatized to Judaism, and therefore was drawn out as a proper person to accuse Paul; and that he was that *Alexander the coppersmith* that did Paul so much evil (2 Tim. iv.14), and whom he had *delivered unto Satan,* 1 Tim. i.20." 3 In other words, some see Alexander in Acts 19 and Alexander in Paul's letters to Timothy as the same person; I tend to agree. In Acts 19:33-34 we see that Alexander was a Jew who gathered together with Demetrius the silversmith in protest against Paul and his companions. Thus, Alexander was a Jew who persecuted Christians. This description matches nicely with how Paul described Alexander the coppersmith in both his letters to Timothy.

In 1 Timothy 1:19-20, Alexander is called a blasphemer who had suffered "shipwreck" concerning the faith. 4 As a result, Paul had delivered him to Satan.

---

1. Prophesied in Matthew 26:64 in fulfillment of Matthew 16:27-28, Daniel 7:13-14, Psalms 110:1 etc.
2. No doubt that Alexander the coppersmith in 2 Timothy 4:14 is the same Alexander mentioned in 1 Timothy 1:20 and Acts 19:33. We will develop this connection further below.
3. Commentary on the Whole Bible by Matthew Henry, p.1715
4. To suffer "shipwreck" concerning the faith suggests that Alexander had at one time professed the faith.

And in 2 Timothy 4:14-15, Alexander the coppersmith 5 had done Paul "much harm" and vigorously opposed his teaching. The similarity of these passages provides solid evidence that Alexander the coppersmith in 2 Timothy 4 was a *Jewish believer turned apostate*, who had become a blasphemer of the church and a persecutor of Christians, particularly Paul. Again, this harmonizes quite nicely with the description of Alexander in Acts 19; he was a Jew and a persecutor of Christians in the first century. Which bring us to our main point.

In the context of the appearing of Christ that was *about to* come, Paul quotes Jesus verbatim and interprets the judgment of Matthew 16:27 to be the judgment that was coming upon Alexander; a judgment *according to his deeds*. Below are the two parallel passages.

> 2 Timothy 4:1,14 (DBY)
> "I testify before God and *Christ Jesus, who is about to judge living and dead, and by his appearing and his kingdom…. Alexander the smith did many evil things against me. The Lord will render to him according to his works.*

> Matthew 16:27-28 (DBY)
> For *the Son of Man is about to come* in the glory of his Father, with his angels, and then *he will render to each, according to his doings…. there are some of those standing here that shall not taste of death until they shall have seen the Son of Man coming in His kingdom.*

Paul is making a truly amazing application. Jesus promised he was "about to come" in the judgment of his persecutors to *repay every man "according to his work"*, and that some of his contemporaries would live to see it. Paul quoting Jesus, prophesied that Christ was "about to appear" to judge the "living and the dead" and Alexander, his contemporary persecutor, would be *repaid "according to his deeds"*. The implication is this: Alexander the coppersmith was about to suffer the vindicatory-judgment, *according to his works*, of Matthew 16:27 for his persecution of the saints at the second coming of Christ *in his own lifetime*. One can only wonder if Alexander, prior to his apostasy, was among "some of those who were standing here" when Jesus spoke those words.

---

5.   The fact that the Alexander in 2 Timothy 4 was a *coppersmith* who did Paul much harm and vigorously opposed his teaching, helps to identify him as the Alexander in Acts 19 and one of the *"workmen of similar trades"* that Demetrius the *silversmith* had gathered together against Paul and his companions in defiance of his gospel. Thus, the Alexander in Acts 19:33-34, 1 Timothy 1:19-20 and 2 Timothy 4:14-15 is one and the same man.

PART III CONCLUSION

As we conclude part III of our investigation, we present a series of comparative charts which illustrate and summarize the ground we have covered throughout this book. As we have demonstrated, several major Old Testament prophecies predicting the covenant return (second coming) of Yahweh, served as the primary prophetic sources for Jesus' prophecy in Matthew 16:27-28. Therefore, *Matthew 16:27-28 prophesied the second coming of Christ in fulfillment of Old Testament prophecy and placed its fulfillment in the lifetime Jesus' generation.*

The first chart below clearly illustrates this truth.

DANIEL 7	ISAIAH 59:17-21	ISAIAH 40:1-10	ISAIAH 62:1-11	MATTHEW 16:27-28
Coming of the Son of Man (7:13,22)	Coming of the Redeemer (59:19-20)	Coming of the Lord (40:10)	Coming of the Lord (62:11)	Coming of the Son of Man (16:27)
Judgment of the Son of Man (7:9,22,26)	Judgment of the Lord (59:18)	Judgment of the Lord (40:10)	Judgment of the Lord (62:11)	Judgment of the Son of Man (16:27)
Coming in glory (7:9,14)	Coming in glory (59:19)	Coming in glory (40:5)	Coming in glory (62:2)	Coming in glory (16:27)
Coming with reward (7:18)	Coming with reward (59:18)	Coming with reward (40:10)	Coming with reward (62:11)	Coming with reward (16:27)
To establish the kingdom (7:14,22,27)	To establish the New Covenant (59:21)	To establish the kingdom (40:9-10)	To establish the kingdom (62:1,2-5)	To establish the kingdom (16:28)
Fulfilled in the "last days" (Daniel 2:28) -parallel text- FIRST CENTURY (Acts 2:15-17)	Fulfilled at the arrival of the New Covenant (59:17-18) FIRST CENTURY (Hebrews 12:18-28)	Fulfilled at the gathering together of Israel (40:9-11) FIRST CENTURY (Matthew 24:31,34)	Fulfilled at the remarriage of Israel (62:2-5) FIRST CENTURY (Matthew 22:1-10)	Fulfilled in the lifetime of Jesus' first disciples FIRST CENTURY (16:28)

We have also demonstrated that Matthew 16:27-28 served as a primary prophetic source for many major New Testament prophesies predicting the second coming of Christ. Therefore, *Matthew 16:27-28 prophesied the second coming of Christ as prophesied in the New Testament, and placed its fulfillment in the lifetime Jesus' generation.*

The next two charts clearly illustrate this undeniable truth.

MATTHEW 16:27-28	REVELATION 19-22	MATTHEW 24-25	MATTHEW 13	REVELATION 1:7
The coming of the Son of Man (16:27)	The coming of Jesus (19:11-13)	The coming of the Son of Man (24:30, 25:31)	The coming of the Son of Man (implied)	The coming of Jesus, coming with clouds
With his angels (16:27)	The armies in heaven followed him (19:14)	Will send forth his angels (24:31, 25:31)	Will send forth his angels (13:31)	The presence of angels is implied (parallel text)
In glory (16:27)	Eyes a flame of fire, on his head many diadems (19:12)	In glory (24:30, 25:31)	In glory (He only comes in glory) (13:30)	With the clouds (the glory-cloud)
To repay every man according to their works (16:27)	To render to every man according to what he has done (22:12)	Judgment of all nations, separation of sheep and goats (25:32)	Judgment of the world, separation of wheat and tares (13:38)	Every eye will see Him, all tribes of the earth will mourn
To establish the kingdom (16:28)	To establish the kingdom (19:15,21:7)	The sheep inherit the kingdom (25:34)	Righteous shine forth in the kingdom (13:43)	To establish a kingdom of priests (1:6-8)
Fulfilled in the lifetime of first century disciples (16:28)	Fulfillment was "soon/near (1:1-3, 22:6-7,10-12)	Fulfilled at the end of the age, in Jesus' generation (24:3,34)	Fulfilled at the end of the age (13:39-40)	Fulfilled in the lifetime of those who pierced him (1:7)
FIRST CENTURY	FIRST CENTURY	FIRST CENTURY	FIRST CENTURY	FIRST CENTURY

MATTHEW 16:27-28	1 CORINTHIANS 15	1 THESSALONIANS 4-5	2 THESSALONIANS 1:4-10	2 TIMOTHY 2-4
The coming of the Son of Man (16:27)	The coming of the Lord (15:23)	The coming of the Lord himself (4:15,17)	The revealing of Jesus from heaven (1:7)	The appearing of Jesus Christ (4:1)
With his angels (16:27)	The seventh (last) trumpet seventh/last angel (15:52)	With the voice of the archangel (4:16)	With his mighty angels (1:7)	Presence of angels is implied-at the judgment
In glory (16:27)	In the glory and image of the heavenly (15:42-49)	In the clouds (glory-cloud) (4:17)	In the glory of his power (1:9)	In eternal glory (2:10)
Judgment according to their works (16:27)	The dead will be raised, we shall be changed (15:52)	At the resurrection, the day of the Lord (4:16, 5:1-2)	To repay with affliction those who afflict you (1:6,8)	To judge the living and the dead, according to their works (4:1,14)
To establish the kingdom (16:28)	To establish the kingdom (15:24,50)	To bring salvation and resurrection (5:8-9)	To reward the saints with the kingdom (1:5,9-10)	To establish the kingdom (2:11-12, 4:1,8)
Fulfilled in the lifetime of first century disciples (16:28)	Fulfilled in Paul's generation - those who were alive would "not all sleep" until the coming of the Lord (15:23,51)	Fulfilled in Paul's generation - some of the living would "remain" until the coming of the Lord (4:15,17)	Fulfilled while the 1st century Thessalonians were still experiencing 1st century persecution (1:6-8)	Alexander was among the generation about to be judged "according to their works" (4:1,14)
FIRST CENTURY	FIRST CENTURY	FIRST CENTURY	FIRST CENTURY	FIRST CENTURY

After a multitude of charts and as many supporting arguments, Matthew 16:27-28 stands tried and tested as one of the most important "prophetic bridges" in all of scripture. This great prophecy identifies the return of the covenant-presence of Yahweh promised in the Old Covenant, *as* the second coming of Christ promised in the New, and places its fulfillment at the end of the Jewish age in AD70.

Having presented and proven our case for the first century second coming of Christ solely from the internal testimony of scripture, we will now support our conclusions from the testimony of first century eyewitnesses.

PART IV

THE HISTORICAL SUPPORT
OF THE
BIBLICAL TRUTH

THE TESTIMONY OF TWO OR THREE
WITNESSES

We are told from scripture that, "by the mouth of two or three witnesses" every matter shall be confirmed. Significantly, this matter itself is confirmed by the testimony of these three witnesses....

> The Prophets:
> A single witness shall not rise up against a man on account of any iniquity or any sin which he has committed; *on the evidence of two or three witnesses a matter shall be confirmed.* (Deuteronomy 19:15)

> The Lord:
> But if he does not listen to you, take one or two more with you, so that *by the mouth of two or three witnesses every fact may be confirmed.* (Matthew 18:16)

> The Apostles:
> This is the third time I am coming to you. *Every fact is to be confirmed by the testimony of two or three witnesses.* (2 Corinthians 13:1)

Furthermore, as we have demonstrated, it is *this threefold witness*, the prophets, the Lord, and his apostles, who testify as one voice to the first century second coming of Christ. In other words, the doctrine of the first century second coming of Christ is biblically confirmed by a biblical threefold testimony. Amazing! Yet despite all this, there are those who say, "that's not enough, we need the testimony of extra-biblical history to *prove* that Christ returned in the first century". As you might sense, there is a fundamental problem with statements like this.

The reality is, no great amount or great lack of uninspired extra-biblical testimony (including church tradition) regardless of how accepted it may be, has the authority to disprove or negate the clear and consistent testimony of inspired scripture. Those who reject the testimony of the bible concerning the first century second coming of Christ based on an *apparent lack* of historical support, have made a fatal mistake. Their reasoning implies that if historical witnesses do not support scripture, then scripture *might not* be true. But this is simply a case of misplaced authority. The bible holds the ultimate authority for biblical truth, not historians.

The fact is, as we have shown above, the bible itself provides a threefold inspired testimony that the second coming of Christ was fulfilled in the first century, in the events surrounding the fall of Jerusalem between AD66-70, and is therefore an undeniable biblical doctrine. Historical testimony can either agree, disagree, or remain silent, but holds no power to disprove or negate the testimony of the word of God. Therefore, by turning our attention to a brief investigation of the extra-biblical record of the first century second coming of Christ, *we do not seek to prove our case from outside the bible, but to simply support and confirm what we have already proven from within it.* As we shall show, the eyewitness testimony of unbiased men entirely agrees with the consistent biblical data and the subsequent logical conclusions we have presented throughout this book.

ANGELIC ARMIES SEEN IN THE CLOUDS
LYAR (APRIL) 21, AD66

Born in Jerusalem in AD37, Titus Flavius Josephus (Yosef ben Matityahu) was a first century Jewish historian and a slightly younger contemporary of the apostles of Jesus. In his first work, a seven-volume account know as "War of the Jews" (AD75-78), Josephus records in detail many events which took place during the Roman-Jewish war between AD66-70. What is so important to remember about the testimony of Josephus is that his writings concerning the war were completed by AD78; less than a decade after the fall of Jerusalem. This tells us at least two things.

One, Josephus' account is taken from actual eyewitnesses, including himself. Two, if his words were not true, that is, if he bore false witness, his contemporaries who were alive to see the same events could have and would have easily refuted his accounts. These facts make the testimony of Josephus and the eyewitnesses he records extremely trustworthy and more than likely, extremely accurate. Please read carefully the following account of Josephus, which he records to have occurred in April AD66, just after Passover.

"Besides these, a few days after that feast, on the twenty-first day of the month Artemisius (lyar), a certain prodigious and incredible phenomenon appeared; I suppose the account of it would seem to be a fable, were it not related by those that saw it, and were not the events that followed it of so considerable of nature as to deserve such signals; for, before sunsetting, *chariots and troops of soldiers in their armor were seen running about among the clouds, and surrounding the cities.*" 1

Now, before we turn to several biblical passages which prophesied this very event, there are several things within this account that are worthy of mention. 2 First, Josephus records the *exact day and the approximate hour* that this took place. It was the *"twenty-first day"* of the month Artemisius, just *"before sunsetting"* (evening). Secondly, Josephus records that at least *two or three witnesses* saw these things take place. He says it was, "related by *those that saw it*". What this means is, we have extremely precise (time specific) eyewitness testimony of two or more witnesses. Therefore, according to the biblical standard for "establishing a matter" laid out by the prophets, the Lord, and the apostles; the testimony of

---

1. Josephus, Wars, 6:296 (6.5.3)
2. For a detailed analysis on these events and more, see Ed Steven's book, *"Final Decade Before the End"*.

these witnesses is established as historical truth. And third, Josephus was most assuredly not attempting to *prove* biblical doctrine, he simply recorded the facts. Notice again what he says, "I suppose the account of it *would seem to be a fable,* were it not related by those that saw it…"

Now remember, Josephus is a Jew who has rejected Jesus as Israel's Messiah, he is not a Christian. This means that he is more than likely unfamiliar with New Testament prophecy. This should help us to understand why Josephus would say that this account could *"seem to be a fable"*. What these witnesses saw and communicated, yet did not understand, was the fulfillment of the second coming (the Parousia) of Christ as prophesied in Revelation 19; a passage which Josephus evidently had not read. If he had, this account would not have "seemed to be a fable", but instead, would have been seen for what it was; the historical fulfillment of John's Apocalypse. 3

This is strong evidence that Josephus was simply stating the facts, not pushing a "preterist agenda", that is, he wasn't trying to build a case for a first century second coming of Christ. With these things in mind, notice the similarities between Josephus and John.

"…. chariots and troops of soldiers in their armor were seen running about *among the clouds,* and surrounding the cities." (Josephus)

> Revelation 19:11,14
> And I saw heaven opened, and behold, *a white horse, and He who sat on it is called Faithful and True,* and in righteousness He judges and wages war…. And *the armies which are in heaven,* clothed in fine linen, white and clean, *were following Him on white horses.*

These Jewish eyewitnesses described the presence of the Lord's army, the host 4 of the Lord, in the clouds of heaven being led by their Captain. This was the beginning of the Parousia, the return of the covenant-presence of Christ (the

---

3. As we shall show, this account of Josephus' was also the fulfillment of Old Testament prophecy. To what extent Josephus connected these miraculous events in Jerusalem to the covenant-return of Yahweh in fulfillment of the prophets is hard to tell. It is probable that he - and others - saw in these events the covenant-judgment of Yahweh, but highly unlikely that they saw in this destruction the promised salvation of Israel.
4. Joshua 5:14

second coming) which began in approximately AD66. 5 John said that the return of Christ was to occur "soon/quickly" from the time he wrote; these eyewitnesses in Jerusalem saw that event begin in AD66. Thus, we have history supporting prophecy.

Yet Revelation 19:11f was not the only prophecy being accomplished. This sighting of Yahweh's angel-army "coming on the clouds" also fulfills the words of Jesus, the New Testament writers, and the Old Testament prophets; whom John was ultimately drawing from in Revelation. Notice again the parallels....

(Josephus)
".... chariots and troops of soldiers in their armor were seen running about among the clouds, and surrounding the cities."

Daniel 7:10,13
A river of fire was flowing and coming out from before Him; *thousands upon thousands were attending Him, and myriads upon myriads were standing before* Him; the court sat, and the books were opened.... I kept looking in the night visions, and behold, *with the clouds of heaven One like a Son of Man was coming..."*

Zechariah 14:5
You will flee by the valley of My mountains.... yes, you will flee just as you fled before the earthquake in the days of Uzziah king of Judah. *Then the Lord, my God, will come, and all the holy ones with Him!*

Matthew 16:27
For *the Son of Man is going to come in the glory of His Father with His angels,* and will then repay every man according to his deeds.

Matthew 24:30-31
"...they will see *the Son of Man coming on the clouds of the sky* with power and great glory. And *He will send forth His angels..."*

1 Thessalonians 4:16,17
For *the Lord Himself will descend from heaven with a shout,* with the voice of the archangel and *with the trumpet of God...* then we who are alive and remain will be caught up together with them *in the clouds..."*

---

5. As already mentioned, the Parousia was not a "twinkling of an eye event". It was a time of *Divine visitation* upon the nation of Israel in both judgment and salvation, and lasted approximately four years (66-70AD), the entirety of the Roman-Jewish war.

1 Corinthians 3:13
So that He may establish your hearts without blame in holiness before
our God and Father *at the coming of our Lord Jesus with all his saints.*

Jude 14
It was also about these men that Enoch, in the seventh generation from
Adam, prophesied, saying, "Behold, *the Lord came with many
thousands of His holy ones.*

Whether they understood it or not, what those eyewitnesses saw and related to
Josephus in AD66 was an undeniable sign that the presence of the Lord had
arrived and the time for Israel's judgment had come. This agrees perfectly with
the *first century time limitation imposed upon each of these texts,* whether explicitly or
implicitly. But the historical testimony of this heavenly omen didn't stop with
Josephus. The first century (AD56-120) Roman senator and historian Tacitus
also records this event. Tacitus, being a contemporary of Josephus could have
easily refuted his record had these events not been true; yet instead he confirmed
it. And, roughly nine hundred years later, the Jewish historian Sepher Yosippon
reiterated these ancient testimonies.

"In the sky appeared a vision of *armies in conflict, of glittering armor".* 6

"Moreover, in those days were seen *chariots of fire and horsemen, a great force flying
across the sky near to the ground coming against Jerusalem and all the land of Judah, all of
them horses of fire and riders of fire."* 7

The parallels between history and scripture are striking indeed. Now, notice the
similarities between Yosippon (above) and Isaiah (below).

Isaiah 66:15-16
For behold, *the Lord will come in fire and His chariots like the whirlwind, to
render His anger with fury, and His rebuke with flames of fire.* For the Lord
will *execute judgment by fire* and by His sword on all flesh, and those slain
by the Lord will be many.

Whether Yosippon understood the implications of his testimony or not, his
account emphatically implied that the heavenly events of the first century were

6.   Tacitus, The Histories, 5.13.
7.   Sepher Yosippon, *A Mediaeval History of Ancient Israel,* (translated from the
     Hebrew by Steven B. Bowman. Excerpts from Chapter 87 "Burning of the
     Temple").

the fulfillment of Isaiah 66. This is crucial, but why? Because, Isaiah 66 was a prophecy of the return of the covenant-presence of Yahweh 8 to establish the new creation. Yet even more than that, Isaiah 66:15-16 was, as we have seen, the prophetic source for the apostle Paul's second coming prophecy in 2 Thessalonians 1. Thus, the historical evidence provides us the testimony of multiple eyewitnesses to the second coming of Christ in the first century, in fulfillment of Thessalonians 1. Notice the parallels between Paul and these Jewish historians....

> 2 Thessalonians 1:6-7
> For after all it is only just for God to *repay with affliction those who afflict you,* and to give relief to you who are afflicted and to us as well *when the Lord Jesus will be revealed from heaven with His mighty angels in flaming fire.*

"Moreover, in those days were seen *chariots of fire and horsemen, a great force flying across the sky near to the ground coming against Jerusalem and all the land of Judah, all of them horses of fire and riders of fire.*" (Yosippon)

"*.... chariots and troops of soldiers in their armor were seen running about among the clouds, and surrounding the cities.*" (Josephus)

Once again, this is history confirming His-story. The first century second coming of Christ is an undeniable historical fact not because history alone says so, but because scripture itself says so, and history undeniably supports that. The following comparative chart powerfully demonstrates the agreement between what these historians say was seen in AD66, and how scripture describes the Parousia event that was going to be accomplished in that generation.

---

8.   In Isaiah 64:1-3 Israel pleaded with the Lord, *"O that you would rend the heavens and come down.... when you did awesome things that we did not expect, you came down, the mountains quaked at your presence."* The reference is to the making of the covenant (giving of the Law) at Mount Sinai (Exodus 19:10-20). At that time, Yahweh "came down". But, his "coming down" was not bodily, it was spiritual; it was the arrival and revelation of his *covenant-presence* with his sanctified covenant people. Thus, the coming of the Lord in Isaiah 66 would be the answer to Israel's plea. The Lord was going to *come down* in the exact same way that he had *come down* at Sinai. The fact that neither Josephus or Yosippon made these connections tells us that neither understood the *nature* of the Messianic kingdom.

THE HISTORICAL TESTIMONY	SEEN BY WITNESSES IN AD66	ELEMENTS OR EVENTS OF THE SECOND COMING	THE BIBLICAL TESTIMONY
Josephus, Yosippon	Chariots	Chariots	Isaiah 66:15
Yosippon	Horses and riders	Horses and riders	Revelation 19:11-14
Josephus	The clouds (glory cloud)	The clouds of heaven	Daniel 7:13, Matthew 24:30 1 Thessalonians 4:17 Revelation 1:7
Josephus Tacitus Yosippon	Soldiers in glittering armor, a great force, heavenly army	Armies of heaven, thousands upon thousands, all the holy saints, mighty angels	Zechariah 14:5 1 Corinthians 3:13, Jude 14 Revelation 19:14
Yosippon	Fire	Flaming fire	Isaiah 66:15-16 2 Thessalonians 1:7
Josephus Yosippon	Surrounding the cities of Judah, coming against Jerusalem	Judgment of Jerusalem (Babylon) destruction of the Jews for shedding innocent blood	Isaiah 66:6,15-16 Zechariah 14:1-5 2 Thessalonians 1:6 Matthew 23:29f Revelation 19:1-3

What was seen by the witnesses in Jerusalem in AD66, was historical extra-biblical proof that the Parousia (the second coming) of Christ was being accomplished at that time. The covenant-presence of Christ in the glory of His Father with his mighty angels had arrived in Jerusalem and all the land of Judah. Rome, as the avenger of God, 9 was used as the instrument of Yahweh to execute his wrath on the nation who had rejected his presence, had persecuted people, and had now become his enemy.

In just a few short years, the once holy city and her once holy children would be completely levelled to the ground leaving not leave one stone upon another, because they did not recognize the time of their visitation. 10 Those were the days of the Lord's vengeance, when all things that had been written were fulfilled. 11

---

9. Romans 13:1-4
10. Luke 19:44 Matthew 24:2-3,34
11. Luke 21:20-22

A VOICE HEARD FROM THE TEMPLE
JUNE AD66 - PENTECOST

Less than two months after the armies of heaven were seen in the sky surrounding Jerusalem, Josephus recorded yet another most remarkable event; this time in the temple. Once again, this historical account is based on the testimony of first century witnesses. In his book, "Wars of the Jews" Josephus says:

"Moreover, at that feast which we call Pentecost, as the priests were going by night into the inner temple, as their custom was, to perform their sacred ministrations, they said that, in the first place, *they felt a quaking, and heard a great noise, and after that they heard a sound as of a great multitude, saying, "Let us remove hence".*
1

Now, notice a few significant points about this ancient account. First, Josephus identifies *the time* that this occurred - the feast of Pentecost, at the hour of the evening sacrifice. Second, he identifies *the exact location* - the inner court of the temple. Third, he records that an audible voice was heard and *the words of that voice were preserved*. And fourth, he clearly *identifies the witnesses* who experienced this event as members of the priesthood. This is obviously an extremely strong testimony, yet we will turn our attention specifically to point number four; the identity of the witnesses. And here's why....

Josephus specifically says it was *the priests* who were going *by night* to perform their sacred ministrations at the *feast of Pentecost,* who experienced this miraculous event. In other words, Josephus didn't just identify these witnesses as "the priests" in general; these witnesses are identified as the specific priests who had ministered in the temple at the time of the evening sacrifice during the feast of Pentecost in AD66. Now that narrows things down significantly; and that's the point. If this event did not happen, then those *specific priests* who had ministered in the temple *at that time* could have easily refuted Josephus's account.

---

1.   Josephus, *The Wars of the Jews*, 1:454 (6.5.3). Much could be said concerning the words, "Let us remove hence", yet we will not do so. We will instead focus on the significance of the voice itself. For some interesting thoughts on the words "Let us remove hence", see Ed Steven's book, "Final Decade Before the End".

Yet so far as we can tell, that never happened. 2 The fact is, the staggering detail in which this event is described provides impeccable credibility to the historical reality of this first century account. With authenticity established, let's now turn our attention to the significance of *the voice* from within the temple.

Just as Israel had missed the connection between the angelic armies in the sky and the fulfillment of Isaiah, they likewise missed it here also. Isaiah prophesied that the Lord would come (return) to Jerusalem in anger and fury to render recompense to his enemies; and that when he did, there would be *"the voice of the Lord from the temple"*. Notice the parallels between Isaiah and Josephus.

> Isaiah 66:6,15
> A voice of uproar from the city, *a voice from the temple, the voice of the Lord* who is rendering recompense to His enemies.... For behold, *the Lord will come in fire and His chariots like the whirlwind..."*

(Josephus)
"Moreover, at that feast which we call Pentecost, as the priests were going by night *into the inner temple*.... and heard a great noise, and after that *they heard a sound as of a great multitude, saying, 'Let us remove hence'"*

Clearly, the event that Isaiah predicted, was the event that Josephus recorded. Isaiah predicted "the voice of the Lord from the temple" at the return of Yahweh (His second coming). Josephus recorded a voice from the temple in AD66. Therefore, what the priests felt and heard in the temple was *proof* that the second coming of Christ to recompense his enemies in fulfillment of Isaiah 66, was taking place at that time. This conclusion agrees perfectly with *when* the second coming of Christ was prophesied to take place; within the lifetime of Jesus' contemporary disciples. AD66 falls within "that generation".

Furthermore, what must not be overlooked is that Isaiah 66 prophesied *both historical events* recorded by Josephus. Isaiah placed both the appearance of the

---

2. Supposing Josephus' account was false, even if the specific priests who had ministered in the temple at that time had not lived through the destruction of Jerusalem to refute it; there is no doubt some of their fellow priests would have. If the account was false, there is no reason to believe that the surviving members of the priesthood would have turned a blind eye to such an outright lie concerning their brethren. In fact, many of the Jews considered Josephus a traitor to the Romans during the war; had Josephus lied, this would have been a perfect opportunity for them to slander his name further.

armies of heaven (seen in AD66) *and* the voice of the Lord from the temple (heard in AD66) at the coming of the Lord. This explains why both events occurred historically within a very short time period. In fulfillment of the same prophecy, *both events* testified to Israel that the covenant-return of Yahweh had begun. Said another way, the first century second coming of Christ was being confirmed by two historical events, through the testimony of "two or three witnesses". By interpreting both historical accounts within the context of Isaiah 66, we see a perfect biblical fulfillment of the second coming of Christ in the first century.

With a shout, 3 and in the presence of his mighty angels, 4 the Lord had "suddenly come to his temple" 5 to execute judgment by fire. 6 And, concerning the *"quaking"* that the priests felt in the temple, this also agrees nicely with Isaiah's prophecy. In Isaiah 64 the prophet recalls the historical events at Sinai when he says, *"You came down, the mountains quaked at your presence"*. 7 As we have shown, the coming of the Lord in Isaiah 66 would occur *in just the same way* that the Lord had "come down" upon Mount Sinai. It makes perfect sense then, why the coming of the Lord to his temple in AD66 was accompanied by "*a quaking*". 8 These manifestations signified that Yahweh had returned to take vengeance on Israel in fulfillment of Isaiah 64-66. But notice what this means:

-The voice in the temple signified the second coming of the Lord in judgment, in fulfillment of Isaiah 66.
-But, the second coming of the Lord in judgment in Isaiah 66 was the Old Testament source for the second coming of Christ in 2 Thessalonians 1.
-Therefore, the voice in the temple in AD66 signified the first century second coming of Christ in fulfillment of 2 Thessalonians 1.

---

3. 1 Thessalonians 4:15-17
4. Matthew 16:27
5. Malachi 3:1
6. 2 Thessalonians 1:6-9
7. Exodus 19:18
8. Although these events did signify the judgment of Israel, the manifestations of *voice and quaking* in the context of the coming of the Lord, also pointed to Israel's covenant-restoration. When the Lord "came down" at Sinai and the mountains "quaked at his presence", Israel was given the Law and established as a covenant people. Similarly, the first century coming of the Lord through the manifestation of *voice and quaking* signified the perfecting a new law, and the establishment of a renewed covenant people.

But again, notice what this means:

-The voice in the temple in AD66 signified the first century second coming of Christ in fulfillment of 2 Thessalonians 1.

-But, Matthew 16:27-28 served as the New Testament source for the second coming of Christ in 2 Thessalonians 1.

-Therefore, the voice heard in the temple in AD66 was proof that the second coming of Christ in fulfillment of Matthew 16:27-28 was historically taking place in the first century, just like Jesus promised.

In conclusion: The extra-biblical accounts of these first century witnesses provide additional support to the inspired testimony of the scriptures. What God has established, history has confirmed. There is but one biblical truth concerning the second coming of Christ: The return of the covenant-presence of Yahweh to accomplish the hope of Israel through the fulfillment of all prophecy, was fulfilled within the lifetime of Jesus' contemporary disciples; as the mouth of the Lord had spoken....

> Matthew 16:27-28
> For *the Son of Man is going to come in the glory of His Father with His angels,* and will then repay every man according to his deeds. Truly I say to you, *there are some of those who are standing here who will not taste death until they see the Son of Man coming in His kingdom.*

CASE CLOSED

MATTHEW 16:27-28
THE SECOND COMING OF CHRIST
FULFILLED IN AD70

The following is a summary of the conclusions we have reach throughout this book, based on our investigation of the biblical and extra-biblical evidence:

1. According to its own context, the coming of the Son of Man in Matthew 16:27-28 would be the vindicatory-judgment of Christ on those who would "take their stand" against the Lord and against his anointed, in fulfillment of Psalms 2 and Psalms 110.

2. Based on their contexts and the eschatological themes found within them, Daniel 7, Isaiah 59, Isaiah 40 and Isaiah 62 all prophesied the second coming of Christ as the covenant-return of Yahweh to Israel.

3. Daniel 7, Isaiah 59, Isaiah 40 and Isaiah 62, *all served as the Old Testament source* for Jesus' prophecy in Matthew 16:27-28. Therefore, Matthew 16:27-28 prophesied the second coming of Christ *in fulfillment of these Old Testament prophecies.*

4. Each major eschatological theme identified within these Old Testament prophesies found fulfillment in the first century, surrounding the fall of Jerusalem in AD70. The *time limitation* imposed upon these prophesies harmonizes perfectly with the first century time limitation that Jesus placed on Matthew 16:27-28.

5. Based on their contexts and the eschatological themes found within them, Revelation 1:7 Revelation 22:12 Matthew 24:30-31 Matthew 25:31f 1 Corinthians 15:51-54 1 Thessalonians 4:15-5:10 2 Thessalonians 1:4-10 and 2 Timothy 4:1 prophesied the second coming of Christ in fulfillment of Old Testament prophecy.

6. Matthew 16:27-28 served as a major prophetic source *for each these New Testament prophesies.* Therefore, Matthew 16:27-28 prophesied the second coming of Christ *in fulfillment of these New Testament prophesies.*

7. Each major eschatological theme identified within these prophesies found fulfillment in the first century, surrounding the fall of Jerusalem in AD70. The *time limitation* imposed upon these prophesies harmonizes perfectly with the first century time limitation that Jesus placed on Matthew 16:27-28.

8. The extra-biblical accounts of multiple first century witnesses concerning two miraculous first century events, support the biblical doctrine of a first century second coming of Christ. Furthermore, the eyewitness testimony of "two or three witnesses" establishes their accounts as legitimate historical truth.

In closing; we have made our Case for the second coming of Christ, and stand firm upon our convictions and conclusions:

Matthew 16:27-28 predicted the second coming of Christ and was in fact accomplished by the fall of Jerusalem in AD70, within the lifetime of Jesus' contemporary disciples. Thus futurism, in all its forms, is completely is falsified.

The reality of the covenant-presence of Christ within his church today neither defers nor destroys the biblical hope of the gospel; instead, it gloriously fulfills it. The essence of walking by faith is refusing to defer what Christ has already fulfilled.

> King Solomon - Proverbs 13:12
> Hope deferred makes the heart sick, but *desire fulfilled is a tree of life....*
>
> Apostle John - Revelation 22:12
> On either side of the river was *the tree of life, bearing twelve kinds of fruit, yielding its fruit every month; and the leaves of the tree were for the healing of the nations.*

As this gospel of fulfillment continues to bear fruit, the fruit of this message will bring healing to the nations. Will you join us?